Amerindian Life and Folklore
(*In Guyana, South America*)

BY

HARRY M. PERSAUD

Publisher: Caribbean Network Enterprise, LLC (CNE, LLC)

ISBN: - 13: 978-1717584199
ISBN: - 10: 1717584195

Amerindian Life and Folklore
(In Guyana, South America)

BY

HARRY M. PERSAUD

2018

Dedication

This book is dedicated to all the Indigenous People of Guyana, among whom I have travelled, sojourned, eaten of their victuals, drunk of their drinks, such as parakari, cassari, warrup, mokororo and biltiri and all the others made of local fruits. I played with their children and listened to their stories, helped work on their plots and slept in their comfortable hammocks.

To the kind boat-captain and the lovely people who I visited on the Rio Branco from Boa Vista to Manaus, I wish to say that I enjoyed their hospitality, engaged in their pastime activities and felt at home wherever I went. I never felt or was I treated as an outsider; neither was I ever made to feel alone.

The Caretakers of the Environment always went out of their way to make me feel comfortable, to explain relationships and sights and sounds which seemed at times to baffle me or which I seemed not to understand. I never forgot one evening when my hunting partner lured a jaguar very near to our wabani then scared the living daylights out of the animal. This happened at Siparuta on the Courantyne River. I thought he meant to shoot it but remembered that the jaguar was a protected animal.

How can one forget such jovial and generous people and not pay respect and homage to their way of life! I dedicate this set of stories to them in grateful thanks for affording me to live for a brief moment in time the life that I love and enjoy best.

Harry Mc D Persaud.

Thanks

Thanks to the persistence of my many friends who have placed their ineradicable trust in me and believed in my capability that I can do it, that I am now putting together a number of experiences and stories that I had already scantily written and which were published in the Guyana Journal.

It is only now that I have convinced myself that these stories will make interesting, informative and educative reading for all those who have never visited the hinterland areas, who have migrated, those who have only received unreliable second versions of a few of these stories, and those inhabitants who think of the narrow Costal Strip of the country as Guyana. I think that it must be known that this view is very limited and does no justice to our history, culture and diversity.

First of all I must thank my nephew, Roop Persaud, for the indefatigable editorial and layout efforts he has put in to make this publication a reality.

To Roop Mohunlall, who was always behind me to get the material published since he saw the collection, I am thankful.

To Dr. Gary Girdhary, who saw the potential, published some of the stories, and gave continued encouragement to me to keep on writing even more.

To all my other friends including but not limited to Charlie, Prof, Rohan and others, who kept on persistently with their encouragement, I say "Thanks guys."

But the greatest encouragement of all was to see the success of my first book in print, *"Why I Have Looked for The Divine and*

What I Have Found", which became a reality because of my nephew, Roop Persaud.

Thanks to Mr. Michael Gomes for his assistance in researching the photographs and for his solicitation of the contribution of Mr. Clyde E. Johnson who designed the cover of this book. All original photographs were supplied by Ms. Jennifer Wishart of Georgetown, Guyana.

To all of you, my friends and well-wishers, I promise to continue writing and, perchance, publishing as the "Cosmic Consciousness" proposes.

H.M.P.

EDITOR'S NOTE: *Perchance it is a first. A person of Indian origin (a PIO) has lived among the Amerindians in Guyana and has been privileged to hear (directly from them) of their oral tradition of passing on their ancestral lore, but, in this case to a "stranger." This "stranger" has written it and it is published by the Caribbean Network Enterprise, LLC. This must be an historic event. But, if it is not, the stories are here committed to paper and print, and, hopefully, they will be preserved. The writer and the editor/publisher shall distribute copies to various public institutions in Guyana and shall be pleased to be assisted by a well-travelled individual of Amerindian descent from the Pomeroon, Essequibo County, one Mr. Ernest Rodie. The editor/publisher acknowledges the contribution of Mr. Michael Gomes who was instrumental in securing original photographs for this publication and for arranging for the art work for the cover design.*

Cover Design By: Clyde E. Johnson of Guyana

(Source for image above: www.en.wikipedia.org identifying Guyana on the continent of South America)

CONTENTS

Names of Settlements I Visited

Encounters

Book Cover: General Design: Clyde E. Johnson of Guyana

The Amerindians of Guyana: An overview of their life

Although human occupation of the Americas dates back to about 12,500 years, the arrival of man into the country of Guyana is of a comparatively recent phenomenon.

It has been proved by Social Scientists that most of the Amerindians who live on the Coastlands and adjoining riverain areas migrated in a series of waves from the Caribbean Islands, possibly from Trinidad, through and over the northern strait which is nearest South America, adjoining the Venezuelan mainland. It is theorized that, from there, they spread to inhabit all the main riverbanks and surrounding areas. These people who comprise the Arawakan line, consist of Warrau, Arawak, Akawoi. Arecuna and Patamona. Pockets of Caribs are found in almost all areas.

It is not known for certain if the inhabitants of the savannah, which forms part of the more extensive llanos of Venezuela, migrated from the upper reaches of the Orinoco, or came through the Takutu and Rio Branco rivers, via the Amazon; but we find this area peopled by the Macushi, Wapishana and Wai-wai. If this is the case, then their origins and subsequent arrival will point to more or less a Peruvian/Incan ancestry. If this is so, they must have left the main body eons ago, since they have brought no technological innovation like terrace farming or a hunting device like the bolas for the capture of animals. This does not, however, offer conclusive proof of their non-Arawakan ancestry and, until ethnological and linguistic research can be done, the origins of the people of the southernmost part of the country will remain shrouded in mystery.

Robert Schomburg, Sir Everard Im-Thurn, Barrington Brown, William Brett Leonard Lambert, Walter Roth, and others, did valuable works. These were done long ago, mostly in the 19th and early 20th centuries. Since then tribes have mingled, some have left, while others were absorbed and thoroughly mixed with others.

For example, the Wai-Wai is the most isolated of the tribes and lived in the remotest parts of the country. They have maintained the peculiar cultural tradition where the males enclose their long hair in a tube hanging down their backs. This was made known to the world when an Englishman published *"Christ's Witch Doctor,"* featuring a prominent picture of the Chief Elka.

The Macushi, on the other hand, who lived mostly in the savannahs bordering the Guyana Shield Formation and riverain areas, will require an expert to tell the difference say, between him and a Patamona.

Students attempting to research these early people may be confused with the early literature, which list as many as thirty tribes. (ImThurn, *"Among the Indians of Guyana', pp 157 - 158")*, but on close scrutiny it will be noticed that the Caribisi, Caribs and Carinja are the same, separated only by peculiar linguistic dialects. A student of Sociolinguistics may easily glean this if he or she takes, for example, the word, "sun". Among the Warrau, the sun is "ya", the Arawaks call it "adali", while the Wapishana and the Atorais call it "kamoo and kamozh" respectively, exhibiting a linguistic affinity. So too do the Carib, Ackawoi and Macushi who call the sun "weya","weyana", and "wey," in that order.

Today nine tribal groups are recognized: Arawak, Arecuna, Akawio, Carib, Macushi, Patamona, Wai-wai, Wapishana and Warrau. They are scattered throughout the country in "reservations" or villages in seventy areas of Guyana. They comprise almost 8% of the population of 750,000, or about 60,000 according to Dr. Odeen Ishmael in his, *"Amerindian Legends,"* (page 9.)

Historians claim that, at the time when Columbus came to the American continent in 1492, there was an estimated population of 70,000 Amerindians in Guyana. It is left to historians and ethnologists to explain the population trend and demise of these people. This in itself will comprise an interesting and useful study in demography and related branches of social science.

At the present time, The Amerindian Act - legislation dating back to colonial times, regulates the lives of these peoples. This Legislation was designed to protect Indigenous Peoples from exploitation. Since Guyana's Independence in 1966, these peoples have been clamoring in an organized way for title to their traditional land holdings. All successive governments agreed to this, but to date, of the 75 villages, only a small part has been demarcated. Some more is promised later, but statistics have not shown that much has been done since and the promise has not been carried out yet in its entirety.

Culture

Most Amerindians still live in the traditional way, depending for their sustenance from the environment. They cultivate their plots some distance away from the village where they have their traditional homesteads. They practice slash-and-burn or swidden agricultural method. Since the nutrients from the cleared fields are soon leached away, they are forced to move from plot to plot, after each cultivation, leaving the abandoned fields to regenerate under natural condition, only returning after a long time - in many instances when the area is unrecognizable from the surrounding untouched vegetation.

The staple among all tribes is cassava. They cultivate the "bitterest" varieties. It must be stated that botanists will tell you that all cassava is bitter, but there are degrees of bitterness among different varieties. It is the bitterest cassava that has the highest concentration of hydrocyanic or prussic acid. If eaten raw, this root can be extremely toxic. Domestic animals have been known to be killed by ingesting this root or drinking its expressed water. This poison however, being a very volatile substance, readily evaporates with the proper application of heat. There are varieties of ways of cooking cassava to make it edible. The very bitter varieties are prepared in a different way from the less bitter. There are people, who are not Indigenous, who avoid planting the very bitter varieties because they cook their cassava differently.

Another important difference is that you do not ever see the bitter varieties exposed for sale in the markets since it is only the Indigenous People who know to make the very bitter varieties safely edible.

The Indigenous Inhabitants grate the bitter cassava on a specially made stone grater and extract the juice out of the mash by using a tubular basket to express the toxic liquid which is caught in a container and which allows the abundant starch to precipitate.

{Above: Amerindian woman with cassava (in her hands), matapi (by her left shoulder), cassava bread and farine (on the log shelf)} Photo Credit: Jennifer Wishart, Georgetown, Guyana

This starch is dried and converted into high-energy Tapioca. The meal is dried over a slow fire and converted to farine and huge cassava bread, which is farinaceous. Once well dried they both have a very extended shelf life. This is the principal bulk-food of the natives. The process of farine making and the making of cassava bread are labor intensive and skillful undertakings. The meal takes a lot of constant turning in the pan on the fire with a special fan and many siftings in specially made sifters. Making of all these implements is the work of the men. Even sifting the starch to make it into granular sago-like consistency takes special skill.

The residual poisonous juice that was expressed from the cassava, having had the sedimented starch removed, is now boiled over a slow fire. The water is boiled until it reaches the consistency of thick molasses. It is now, dark brown and has miniature crystalline grains, which takes special effort to discern. This is the most famous occidental sauce known as "casreep."

Many other sauces are sold under the name of "casreep", but there is no substitute for the real thing, and though many outsiders are fooled with substitutes like caramel and the so called "coconut casreep", only the real thing can truly titillate the taste buds of those who know "the real mc-coy."

A variety of food crops are planted: gourds and pumpkins, yams and the native and peculiar mauve potato, (confined to the forested regions outside the Rupununi area), sugar cane, tannias and yams, cucumbers and melons and maize and tomatoes.

In the Rupununi, and along the galleria forests along the rivers, there are numerous ite trees. These trees bear a tangerine-size, dark-brown, rough, purple fruits in huge bunches. Between the rough rind and the huge seed is found about an eighth to a quarter inch oily pulp, which is rich in nutrients. When ripe these fruits are harvested, steeped in warm water for some time and the delicious meat is extracted and made into orange sized balls, which are eaten or sold. These are mixed with water and seasoned and made into a very delicious drink. Although this is not a practice of inhabitants of the forested regions, it is quite common in the savannas.

The ite swamps also serve as the open sties to keep their semi-feral pigs, which they hunt whenever they need communal meat or in times of scarcity. Most villages make this a habit, to have such stocks.

All the tribes make intoxicating beverages from the products in their environment. Cassiri, parakari, and cassava-wine are made from the burnt cassava flour from the pans of the cassava bread. These are the well-known cassava drinks. One widely spread one is the fermented juice of the sugarcane, locally known as warrup. (I have even drunk warrapa and eaten coi, "giunea-pig", in Peru). The mauve potato among the forested tribes are boiled and fermented and made into an intoxicating drink called "bilteri". Moco-moco in the Rupununi is famous for corn-wine, while the mokororo, made from cashew, is well known by all who has ever tasted it.

In remote times salt was a prized commodity and was an item of trade. This was obtained in two ways. The people of the savannah and interior areas used to burn the pith of the ite palm and collect the mineral residue, while at other times other shallow lacustrine areas provided this commodity when water evaporated and left a crystalline brown saline crust.

Protein was obtained, and still is, by fishing the multitudinous streams and lakes. The natives have adopted a variety of methods, including poisoning with plant narcotics, blocking and bailing, using fish-traps, spring hooks, night fishing with lights and spears and machetes.

Hunting is still done in the forests and savannahs along with slaughtering some of the pigs that they tend in the ite swamp. In the remote areas where money forms an infinitesimal part of the economy, both the farms and the swine in the swamps are owned communally. Produce from the farm, along with the dressed meat, is shared among the households. Produce from the farms, along with the hunted and dressed meat, is distributed equally according to need. Meat and fish are either preserved by roasting and smoking over a slow fire, or by boiling the meat in casreep and peppers in a pot to which fresh meat is added as often as it is required or obtained.

Clothing, which was all formally made by the women, represents the exotic concept of the people that we see in books and magazines, inserted for purposes best known to the writers. Now-a-days, at places as remote as Konashen and Baramita, the people wear western clothes, which they got through bartering or buying.

(Above: children in traditional dress)
Photo Credit: Jennifer Wishart, Georgetown, Guyana

(Above: adult in "western" clothes)
Photo Credit: Jennifer Wishart, Georgetown, Guyana

For sleeping, all the tribes use hammocks made by hand. Some are made with "tibisiri" (the spun raffia part of the ite leaves) while people of the savannah hand make the best cotton hammocks in the world. Owning one costs much.

The homes in the forests usually have open sides thatched with palm leaves. Many of them have a central room for privacy. In the permanent villages the houses are walled with the outer layer of the palms and may have openings for windows. Some have shutters.

The savannah, to my mind, has the most sensible houses in the entire country. They are built with adobe walls and thick ite roofs. These houses are cool during the hot noonday sun and warm during the nights. Where houses are not of this vintage they need fans during the day and heat at nights.

Before European penetration, the Peiman was the most respected person, next to the captain, among the tribes. He acted as medicine man, confidante and philosopher. While the captain administered to their physical wants, the Peiman was doctor and psychologist.

Next was an unknown personage known as Kanaima. Whether in natural or spiritual form, he acted, as the social conscience to keep wrongdoing in check, since, to offend any member, was to surely bring down the wrath of Kanaima, which will result in inexplicable sickness or even death.

The advent of "civilization" saw many natives converted to Christianity, chiefly Roman Catholicism in the savannahs, and Seventh Day Adventist in the Coastal and a few mountain areas. However some of the inhabitants evolved their own brand of religion, which combined both Christianity and their own tenets, and created a peculiar brand of Christianity, later known as the Hallelujah Religion. This is gradually being replaced by Christian orthodoxy.

Much literature exists on puberty, child bearing and funeral rites. Suffice it to say that only in the remotest parts are these observed, since more has succumbed to the more acceptable national standards in these social behaviors.

In sports, while traditional wrestling occurs mostly on unplanned occasions, many of the males indulge in cricket and football and "rounders" in most village squares. The traditional style in walking in Indian file can be found in almost amongst everyone. Even the few Coastlanders who take up government jobs in remote areas fall in line when travelling on foot.

It is still not strange to notice a man and his wife walking as a couple, travelling on foot, with the male in front with his gun, or bow and arrow, and the female some distance behind, laden down with a full warashi. In some settlements can be found the occasional SUV, or sometimes a bullock cart. The latter is a peculiar contraption where the wheels are fixed to the axle. The axle spins instead of the wheels around a fixed axle. The whole contraption of axle and wheels spins about two vertical planks nailed to the cart. Most of the villages have schools where English is taught, but in many areas and villages, the native language is spoken at home. Before the advent of Coastlanders, who speak broken English, it was not strange to find all the children speaking perfect Standard English as taught by the Missionaries. Even today it is little known, but it is not strange to find in places like the Lethem area, children and adults speaking their native language along with Spanish, Portuguese and English.

Many Amerindians have arisen to positions of prominence. Stephen Campbell, of Arawakan extraction, was a legislator and Minister of Government. His daughter, Ms. Viera, was a schoolteacher and today an activist for her people. Umblita Van Sluytman copped first from among a bevy of Guyanese beauties to represent Guyana in England in an International Beauty Pageant. Michael Gomes became Regional Education Officer. There are many medexes, or barefoot doctors, who are serving their communities with distinction. With few exceptions, all the Captains of the villages are Amerindians, or of Amerindian extraction. The Co-op Officer of Region 9 is a Chinese trained functionary, Mercier

Baretto. All fields of endeavor will see Amerindians filling top positions and other important posts. Amerindians are the greatest assets to the research biologist, both local and foreign, since they know the extensive flora and fauna by their individual names, and they can lead an expedition unerringly through numerous byways and paths that crisscross the terrain.

If I am any authority, may I mention that the most astute person that I have encountered is a full-blooded Wapishsna who was the wife of the Lethem Medex. She was so astute that she quickly solved problems that needed solutions while her lettered companions were still mulling over the preliminary information.

With the advent of outside incursion many "natives" have been brought into a moneyed economy, which has changed their lifestyle somewhat. Many are the times when they earn hard dollars by hard and protracted toil, they quickly spend the money with willful abandon on trifles and nonessentials; and so will either have to revert to the farm or leave home again to earn sustenance.

Since it is the males that go out to work, they employ the grubstaking method where they will take things from the village shop on credit, which they are hardly able to work out. So they continue owing and being beholden to the shops and merchants. Most times it is the shop-owner or the merchant that owns the means of employment.

It once happened a little time before I was there that the people were encouraged to plant carrots, peanuts and potatoes. This they did with the concomitant neglect of their traditional cassava fields. Peanuts and carrots were left in storage because of lack of transportation. Tomatoes shared the worst since they started to rot because of a lack of cold storage. The farmers lost their entire livelihood and, to make it worst, they had to buy foreign food.

Seventeen years ago, in 2000, it was designated National Amerindian Year in Guyana where the history and culture of the people were highlighted and given prominence. But History and Culture are poor substitutes to share out to disadvantaged and hungry children. All the lands were not yet titled.

I have friends that feel that the Indigenous Peoples should not be brought into the mainstream Guyanese life. This is the worse-case scenario that I have heard to date. There should be no debate that they should be brought into mainstream life as soon as possible and afforded all possible means to gain lucrative and sustainable employment. It is the bounded duty for any government and this matter should be made a priority.

From Day One a Ministry should have been created to facilitate this. We cannot afford to marginalize any section or sector of our population, much less the original inhabitants of our land. This creates niches and pockets of inequality, and, where this is based on Culture and ethnicity adumbrating spurious unscientific and selfish reasons, it will create niches of cultural inequalities, which tend more to marginalize rather than to integrate. Their culture and ways of living have much to offer modern life to make it more comfortable than running headlong into a moneyed economy with all its greed, pitfalls and disequilibration of inequality and distribution of goods and services to the detriment of some who are not the shakers and movers of society.

It is rumored that Guyana will benefit from huge oil finds come 2020. I am yet to see Indigenous representation made for their rightful share of this largesse. It is my thesis that they are being left out in the rush for a countrywide claim of the patrimony, which is rightfully theirs.

For our native peoples to share in what is rightfully theirs need the help of International Organizations. Widespread and in depth studies and recommendations are urgently needed to see that an equitable distribution of any of the resources of Guyana are preserved and managed for the benefit for all its citizens.

Carrying schools to these people is not the best method to educate them. Rather more successful methods ought to be found. They must also be taken to schools outside their environ, be trained, and, with dedicated mentors sent to modern facilities to teach their peoples. This is a small part and only an infinitesimal part of the solution. No one likes to stay isolated. Therefore industries must be opened up to propel the various areas into the 21st. century, economically, so that there shall be little difference in amenities and conditions for modern living among the various communities and their peoples.

An attempt was made once by the Royal Agricultural and Commercial Society during colonial times to continue the works of Im Thurn and others through philanthropy and their magazine, "Timehri", which at least highlighted the social conditions of the native peoples and so garner sympathy for their economic and other conditions, but this organization was elitist and soon died out. This organization must still have in its archives valuable information that can serve as a springboard to initiate modern research complementing what has gone before, and what has been done since then, and what needs to be done to propel our most vulnerable inhabitants successfully into the 21st. century so that they can share equally in the resources of our homeland.

(Above: lone Amerindian child going to school in a canoe. Photo credit: Jennifer Wishart, Georgetown, Guyana) Note back-pack

Under A Rupununi Sky

It was 'The Bard of Avon' who once said, "There is a tide in the affairs of men, which taken at the flood leads on to fortune. Neglected, all their efforts are bound in shallows and in misery".

Having been in various senior, but acting positions, at my place of employment for fourteen years in the same school and could not be made permanent in any of the acting positions although suitably qualified, I was feeling frustrated and psychologically stagnated. This should not have been, but the country's political climate was such that, handpicked persons, who were of a particular political persuasion, were promoted. I was not singular in that respect. Others found it difficult to be upwardly mobile although they were amply qualified. However, political patronage, rather than seniority, ability, and suitability mattered more.

Since "party boys" headed all the schools on the Coastland, I decided to apply for a school in the hinterland area. I applied in July to be Head of two interior schools. It is customary that vacancies be filled in time for the reopening of schools in September. I became very despondent when September came and one of the schools I applied for was given to one of my juniors, both in qualification and experience. The other school, I was told, was not vacant although it was advertised as such. The truth of the matter was that transfer of a Minister of Government fell through and, since his wife was Head of the school for which I had applied for, it did not become vacant as anticipated. The Minister, having been transferred at a later date, his wife could not remain alone, so she also had to be transferred. So it happened, that on January 13th I received a letter from the Teaching Service Commission, by courier, appointing me as Head of St. Ignatius Community School, the other school for which I had applied.

I asked for a week to co-ordinate and conclude some personal business, and it was granted. So, exactly seven days later I was on a D C 3 aircraft winging my way en route to the Interior. The flight, though uneventful, was very interesting. One only had to look through a window to see, punctuating the lush verdure of the forest, newly cut and burnt clearings, some still smoking from the unfinished burnt heaps, with the smoke curling and twisting still, yet with scattered cumulus cloud islands adorning the horizon as far as the eyes could see. Some clearings distinguished themselves by displaying young growth that was cultivated the previous year, being distinctly different from the drab columns of the forest. Others again displayed old growth now rejuvenating to their former glory. An astute traveler with a keen sense of geography would notice the difference in vegetation, and recognize, in the distance, how this is different from some rain-shadow areas or may be able to discern the differences in elevation, by the change in vegetational patterns.

The easily recognizable savannahs soon appeared. This phenomenon, the savannah, is really a part of the great Venezuelan llanos that stretch between the Roraima formation and the Acarai Mountains. In Guyana it is gently rolling both in the North savannahs and the South savannahs, which are slightly unequally divided by the Kanuku Mountains. Both savannahs in Guyana extend for over three hundred miles with myriads of streams penetrating the flat land and draining into the tributaries of the Amazon, the Essequibo and other minor rivers. To see the lush verdant valleys of the Kanuku penetrating the brown savannahs and snaking among them is to experience an acute sense of impending adventure among the most uninitiated. What was interesting to me and represented a sort of anomaly was that only one mountain peak of this great range is in Brazil - The Toucano. This mountain was devoid of any greenery. These savannahs and the entire area are so interesting that they attracted a Cambridge University Study, the findings of which are in The University of Guyana.

After a hardly noticeable hour and fifteen minutes we made a perfect three-point landing on the smooth airstrip of Lethem. This is the largest airstrip in the entire region and was in good repair and constantly upgraded.

(Above: Town of Lethem, Guyana: Source: The Guyana Chronicle)

The settlement, or township, of Lethem is conveniently located at the confluence of the Moco-moco and Takutu rivers, with the green and majestic Kanuku mountains forming a beautiful backdrop as if on an Oriental tapestry. It is nearly in the center of the savannahs. The region boasts a modern abattoir, which form the hub around which the population is concentrated. This township is the headquarters of the entire region and has all the important government facilities.

As the Kanuku is green and lush among the brown savannahs, so too appear the contrast in housing, which the Moco-moco divides. Lethem proper has all of the government administrative buildings and a prominent supply store. On the other side of the river is St. Ignatius where the bulk of the local people live in adobe houses covered with ite palm leaves. On this side are two exceptions in the Community School and teachers' houses built of modern materials and, the priest's "mansion " built at two stories with adobe, but neatly plastered with cement so as not to be recognizable as adobe. It is, nonetheless, covered in asbestos sheets. Many of the

22

houses in Lethem sport a few decorative herbiage, but this is absent in St. Ignatius. There are also the nurses' quarters of one storey in Lethem, but an imposing mansion easily dwarfs these, which was the domicile of the former governor of the area during Colonial times.

The town of Lethem is named after the former governor, Sir Gordon Lethem KCMG. I doubt that anyone living today remembers the original name of "Arewa". The old Touchau who was seeing an erosion of the culture and the old ways disappearing before his very eyes as the younger generation ape the ways of the Coastlanders and only adopt the malign patterns that are replacing their traditional behavior, intimated this to me.

The climate of the savannah teetered somewhat between the extremes diurnally especially during the hot months. Climatically, there is one long dry season and one wet one. Being far away from any cooling moisture-laden clouds near the ocean, the little that form seemed to easily dissipate during the night and so terrestrial heat readily escapes and the nights get cool to cold readily. So, there is a great daily fluctuation. This however is greatly tempered by the sensible houses of the locals which keep cool during the day because of the thick thatch and adobe walls and which keep warm during the cool nights because of the insulating powers of the housing materials. This is exactly the opposite with concrete walls and galvanized roofs, which readily gain and lose heat or cold.

Other cultural differences may be noticed between the food consumed by the two sets of inhabitants.

Although the country is ranch land, (an imported activity to the area), there is a conspicuous absence of milch cows. Feral Texas longhorns are reared for beef, which provides the principal export of the Region. Milk is principally used by the Coastlanders and is provided by the general store in the form of imported powdered milk and evaporated forms imported from a country outside Guyana.

The employment pattern further exacerbates social distinction. All the technical and high paying jobs are not only open to outsiders but are occupied and many kept open to them only. When a vacancy occurs people are imported into the area. The menial, more physically taxing and low paying available positions, are occupied by the natives both at the abattoir and in government institutions.

The local High School was staffed exclusively by outsiders with even a Welsh social Studies Head of Department. And, to make it worse still, plans were afoot to import and employ two Sri Lankan Specialists to man this Department. This was forestalled because of lack of knowledge of the local history and culture of the local inhabitants. The Kindergarten and Grade School Sections were staffed nearly entirely with importees. Needless to say that all the senior positions were held by outsiders.

The literature concerning communication with the local inhabitants embraces two schools of thought, according to which one one was exposed to. Writers who actually spent a long time among the locals have found them to be open, astute, intelligent, perceptive and jovial, while others have written of them as people who are secretive, (even with their names), and simple and childish in demeanor. However, I feel that, honesty, and honesty of purpose, is readily discerned by the locals in that this is the key ingredient to breeding trust for, especially, strangers. This trust, which is the key ingredient in eliciting the normative behavior of not only a person, but also people in general, must be cultivated and adhered to for any successful living. This writer feels that any population anywhere in the world is of the same basic behavior in all the genetic categories and the baser categories, which are the result of abberative conditions. But this might not be strictly in concordance with environmental influences. Love is shown where love is given or earned while distrust and envy are more a product of abberative stimuli. I am however a firm believer in the bell-curve distribution for any homogenous population.

Almost every Amerindian knows to communicate in four languages. English taught in schools, the native Wapishans and Macushi taught from the cradle, and Spanish/Portuguese that happen to be the language of the border. Is it then not myopic and anomalous and not in consort with the culture of the people that English is the only language taught in school?

During my sojourn, there was a feeling that most of the people, despite their employment ties, were more closely affiliated to the inhabitants across the border than their fellow Guyanese. In fact there were some people who actually lived in Brazil who occupied high positions at the stock-farm and abattoir and, one, even a government position. It must be noted that during the now infamous "Rupununi Uprising", many, even Guyanese of Caucasian decent, escaped across the border never to return.

During my stay there, there was an attempt to diversify the agricultural base with an accent on peanuts, carrot and tomatoes. This had a twofold disastrous effect on the native population. First, no red-blooded native will eat rice once there is farine. I even had a security guard whose wife will cry bitterly if she could not get her farine to eat, and so flatly refused to eat rice. Second, the cultivation of the peanuts, carrots and tomatoes led to a neglect in the cultivation of cassava, which formed their basic staple food. This led to untold hardship and near starvation when they could not get their new products to markets on the Coastlands. The products spoiled and rotted at the depot. The tomato became ketchup before they reached the airstrip because of rough terrain, and the larders were left at home empty and they had no money in their pockets to buy the foreign foods. Even the little that was sold to local outsiders was grossly inadequate to purchase anything substantial.

To be fair it must be noted that, as the people have been catapulted into a moneyed economy, many squandered their cash on non-essentials and so suffered the consequences. But most of all, there was the sudden disequilibration of cultural practices, which led into uncertainty and thus gave rise to unknown and disastrous consequences with unknown results, which took many years to rectify.

Having set the stage of the milieu into which I had opted to go in perspective, I will now state that it was one of the best decisions I have ever made. What was gained and what is left with me are so ineradicably imbedded in my very being that, if re-incarnation is true, these feelings, impressions and behavior will surely be taken beyond the grave.

I do aver categorically that I have not met a more genuine set of people ever, anywhere. Lying is anathema to the majority of them. Keeping to their word, to them, their word is as sacred as the omnipotent One, to whom they give their belief. No one, especially a stranger, is allowed to leave the most humble of homes without having something to eat. For that matter, on the humblest table is a container mixed with farine and tapioca, which anyone can dip his hand into anytime. And, since mealtime is anytime, a stranger is promptly handed a cup with water, sugar and a spoon to have some. Length of stay is not asked, and length of stay can last as long as one wants to stay providing assistance is given with daily chores and the other activities that go with the lightening of the burden of daily living. There is always a spare hammock and accommodation at the hearth of the least affluent. The love of children is phenomenal. For my continuous three years of residence among these people I have never witnessed them administering corporeal punishment for any infraction, regardless of its severity or gravity.

Among the native inhabitants I was privileged to be associated with, in my PTA, a woman in the personage of the wife of the Medex. She was a committee member. She was unlettered and in her own words "...did not go far in school." However, when complex decisions were to be made, or an especially complex problem was to be resolved, her solutions were invariably the ones to be accepted without the least discussion. Not only was she pragmatic, quickly utilizing a holistic approach, but also will quickly and astutely suggest that a desired line of action be used. I always wondered what would have been the position if, "... knowledge, rich with the spoils of time," was allowed to unfold in her case! And if it did unfold wholly in her favor, what if she was allowed to go far in school? On my frequent visits to the city I never failed to discuss her with my professional colleagues. She impressed me so much that I regard her as a prodigy, "born to waste her sweetness on the desert air".

Even the casual visitor to this area will not fail to notice the impact that the Missionaries have on the native population. Apart from the change wrought in their beliefs, the Church is also active in the area of family values, morality and other Christian etchant values.

One of the strongest men is one I have seen in this area. Despite of his frequent imbibition of parakari, he maintained a superb physique and can effortlessly lift the entire end of a Land Rover. I have seen him do it many times without a dare. It was a sad day when his own bullock cart toppled over him as he descended a steep incline while returning to Lethem from a manore and killed him.

I had a High School student who ran seven miles to school every morning, rain or shine and was never late. He even ran home during the hottest part of the day. I have seen on certain Saturday nights, entire families - father, mother and children ranging from six years old to tiny tots, seated in line in a discotheque, and the father having taken a drink of some mildly intoxicating beverage, give the wife a drink, and in turn give each of the children. Was this love, or child abuse? It is not for me to judge.

I have witnessed rodeos, as skillful as any in the American West, being performed by barefoot cowboys called vaqueros. These rodeos became an annual feature and attracted cowboys from ranches on the Coastland.

Observing the landscape while walking with a family to the foothills of the Kanuku is an experience never to be forgotten. Walking in the early morning with the dew glinting from the every exposed blade of grass, sparkling like diamonds, has to be seen to be appreciated.

Meandering among the stunted sandpaper trees (Curatella Americana) and being rasped by the leaves, one is left to wonder what gave them such a unique quality and texture. The tree is a product of pyroclasticity and, as always, survives the numerous fires set intentionally or otherwise in the savannah during the dry season. One will be thrilled by the abundance of wildlife scurrying among the crispy leaves under the trees, or the turtle and Barbary doves busily scratching and searching for seeds in the nooks and crannies of the poor lateritic soil. Or, if one were to lift one's eyes and gaze in the distance, one would observe flocks of trogons and troupials circling and bothering insects over the dark green tops of the taller trees. One can go on and on tirelessly describing the natural wild beauty of the landscape, but any amount of verbal description will do injustice and be inadequate to describe the beauty and tranquility. There is no other parallel biome on the planet to compare to a llano in transition to foothills.

Although some, out of ignorance and maybe ungrounded dislike, have sometimes, in lean years, categorized some areas as "Chattos Land", one only has to explore and cultivate the valleys of the foothills of the Kanuku to find out the extreme fertile nature of the soil which is perpetually being nourished by the constant leaching of the minerals from the mountains. One wit, who was very knowledgeable about this once remarked, "... even a dwarf would get taller if he stands on the rich soil of the foothills of the Kanuku long enough". This fact has been borne out by the many successful farmers who continue to cultivate the same area in the foothills throughout their lives without moving out of the areas. The most important part of my stay ought to be my job and this was so.

It took dedicated teachers to leave home and family and the comforts and amenities of the Coastlands to work so far away from homes, knowing that in an emergency it may take many days to be reunited with the family. In my experience everyone was totally immersed in his/her vocation. Even among the inadequately qualified were found a commitment and dedication rare even among their qualified peers. Lack of academic qualification was adequately made up for with the unstinted dedication and co-operation displayed by most. Among the fifty odd schools of the Interior Region our school alone produced half of the Interior Scholarships. These were students who did well in the SSEE to merit places in prestigious secondary schools in the Capital City.

Children are the same everywhere if presented with the same opportunities. Suffice it to say that most of these students I was privileged to encounter were a set in whose veins there was art. Sad to say that the only school that was to cater for such talent had not one iota of a Fine Arts Program. Neither was singing, painting, dancing, music or theatre. Yet when Outsiders were invited to visit the region, (during my stay), students were required to greet them at the airport with cultural renditions, being it a school day or not. Many used to take umbrage, but persuasion, fear of reprisal and the innate need to please, obliged those concerned even to take students into their homes to meet these "anomalous activities." I especially remember Carol and Frankie "Dry Run Slowe" who always insisted that there must always be a "dry-run" before presentation. Thanks to them and others things always fructified to the satisfaction of all.

Being extremely mannerly and courteous, with little or no distraction, the children developed extended attention span, which morphed into making teaching an extreme pleasure. Teachers did not have to frequently interrupt the teaching process to have ordered activity or discipline. Teaching was a pleasure. This does not say that the students displayed blankness of behavior. Rather they asked the same relevant questions as their attentive peers anywhere would do. An observant teacher can distinguish understanding or pleasure or puzzlement in the students' visages as he teaches. Rules, once discussed and made, were adhered to and a teacher will hardly find a child asking an irrelevant question that may suddenly pop into his/her head.

Because of the peculiar climatic conditions of the area and usually absentee parents, (who may be at their farms in the foothills), the school held double sessions and sent the students home during the hottest part of the day. Frequently the temperature soared over one hundred degrees during the dry season. It stands to reason that, if one eats during this time, somnolence steps in and the teaching-learning process ceases, or at least, wanes. Sometimes the cooling breezes sweep across the savannahs and encourage the students who live nearby to remain in the schoolyard to play.

All the children love to play games. During any season, some, both boys and girls, may be seen playing soccer in the schoolyard. They need no supervision, and will play indefatigably for hours until darkness will force them to retire to their homes.

One could have taught any number of years in this idyllic and conducive environment among such wonderful people. I had secretly vowed to spend at least five years when I would have had ample time to see the fruits of my labor, when the students I would have taken in at Form One, having run the entire gamut of my whole program and methodology and receiving my reward after five years, in the results of external Examinations. But this was not to be. [The entire story is told in the book *"Why I Have Looked For The Divine And What I Have Found." Amazon.com*]. But, like the Coastland, politics played an important part in my keeping my job.

Questions like, "Why should the Headmaster fraternize more with the down trodden or the Church? Why does not the Headmaster keep closer to the Coastlanders than to be made more familiar with government's policy, etc.?" are of no use. To my mind the natives needed me more than the political hierarchy and, most of all, I love their story and mode of living.

After a sojourn of more than three years, I was virtually kicked out of the region - in the words of The Regional Chairman, "For carrying out "apolitical" (sic) activities, and keeping the wrong company".

Today, I look back with nostalgia and hope one day to return. My greatest, most impressionable and fondest memories, still linger under the Kanuku clouds where, according to legend, "dreams are realized".

(Above: the 'idyllic' Kanuku Mountains, Guyana. Source: www.blogconservation.org)

****

Mashramani: *The Concept*

Though it is over fifty years ago, it seemed like it was just yesterday I was paddling up the placid waters of the Supenaam Creek accompanying my stepfather to Bethany Mission. This was because of an invitation from the Captain of the Mission.

My stepfather worked, for the most part of his life, with and among the natives of the river. So it was not surprising when he received an invitation to join the people of the Mission in their unique celebration.

It was just after the big rains in June-July when the entire population embarked on the project to rebuild the old school building. My stepfather decided that I should accompany him since he felt that the exposure would be a new learning experience for me. There were few outsiders except the white Priest of the Mission, and the Headmistress, my stepfather and I.

Mash-a-muni

Although shy and apprehensive at first I felt honored to be exposed to and to be a part of something new, which, until now, seemed remote and alien to what I have been accustomed. In later years I was very fortunate to, not only share in such celebrations, but also to be an active participant in many projects and activities of a similar nature.

Using the tide to speed us along we arrived well in advance of the commencement of the ceremony. I learned from mingling with the various groups (I had to play it by ear), that the undertaking was Mash-a-mu-ni. My stepfather had hinted the word to me, but his pronunciation of it seemed a bit different from what I was hearing.

After the villagers finished rebuilding the school, the men left early in the evening on various expeditions to hunt meat for the communal pot for the day after. The women, meanwhile, had prepared a huge amount of cassava bread (kali). Two barrels of cassiri had been set the week before and were strained and put into enamel buckets. Gourds of fermented potato drink (bilteri) and cane wine (warrup) were also prepared and placed on a long wooden platform in the schoolyard.

(Above: pepperpot stew – an Amerindian meat dish - Source: www.npr.org)

When the men arrived with the meat - two capybaras, three labbas and a tapir - the women got down to business and, before long, had chunks of meat boiling vigorously away in casreep. On top of this appetizing sauce floated a number of red, yellow and green whole chili peppers. To the uninitiated the contents of the boiling pots looked black and unappetizing, but the deliciously pungent aroma belied the appearance The entire area was engulfed in such an aroma that this seemed to slow down the sun which dimming will herald the lighting of the bon-fires and initiate the commencement of the ceremonies.

All these activities with their attendant sights and sounds proceeded at a leisurely pace without any fuss like a well-oiled machine. Everyone seemed to know what was required and got about doing it in the right time and in the right order. There was positively no confusion, which seemed to have been the case of similar rites.

As I circulated among the various groups, I seem hardly to notice that the men were now dressed in colorful shirts and plain trousers that were neatly pressed. The women at this stage occupied themselves with preparing of or setting of the food and drinks on the long wooden table.

At the setting of the sun, four huge bon-fires were lit at the four corners of the square in the sandy schoolyard. The Priest stood at a small table, which stood at one side and was covered with a white cloth with a glass vase with some water, which was accented with the biggest variegated orchid I had ever seen. The scene was surreal and, to some, might have resembled a primitive Holy ceremony with the attendant set of pagans indulging in some ancient ritual. The priest, with his flowing attire, called the people to order and lauded the captain and all those who were responsible to bring such a useful project to a successful fruition. Among other things he enumerated the benefits that will accrue to the village as a whole. They must make good use of the facility and use it to further the work of the Lord.

The Headmistress congratulated everyone and thanked all, especially the women, to have brought the occasion to the success it was. The Captain, in flawless English, made a short speech in which he pledged his unstinted and continued support of all that will benefit the village in the future.

The females were now attired in beautiful print dresses and looked like pretty pictures.

The real celebration then began. To the music of two drums, a tambourine and several improvised instruments and a guitar, the women faced the men in a line and stamped and swayed to the music - in a circle and square dances. The atmosphere would have surely given an outsider the impression of a primitive pagan ritual being enacted on the white sands with the huge bon fires and the people costumed as they danced and swayed to the mesmerizing beats. After a little moment there was a lull when the Captain took a huge bowl of cassiri, took a deep draft and handed it to the priest who did likewise and handed the bowl to my stepfather who took a draft and passed it to the next person. And so it went. These sour-sweet slightly intoxicating liquors were being drunk from communal bowls. After a time the women then shared in the bilteri but the men continued drinking the cassiri and warrup. After a time the priest, captain and my stepfather took huge bowls of pepperpot and cassava bread and started the feasting. This became a peaceful free for all. People ate as much as they could have possibly done. This made some sleepy while pockets of people did as they wanted. They ate, sang, danced and ate to their hearts' desire until most were over satiated. My stepfather and I were given two hammocks in an open hall adjoining the Captain's house. I was soon overcome with sleep and soon relaxed in the arms or Orpheus.

So, this was *Mashramani!* This, "all for one and one for all'! This camaraderie, this co-operation made an indelible impression on my memory, which is as vivid today as it was over sixty years ago.

As I grew up, I wondered why we of the Coastlands of Guyana did not do likewise to make something, the tasks of which require many hands, may be executed and expedited for the good of all. Later, I discovered that at certain times there was a degree of co-operation among the farmers during rice cutting and rice planting time, but the celebration at the conclusion was anything but lavish.

Kayap

The word registered vividly in my mind but I did not have even a slight understanding of what it was. In the early years of my teaching career, while I was a guest of a contemporary in the Pomeroon River, my host and I were invited to a Kayap. The word sounded strange and so did not awaken any mental pictures in my memory of my past experiences. Imagine my surprise when I was confronted with the same type of scenario as that of my experience in the Supenaam River! But this time the occasion was the completion of the cutting down an area of land on which an individual will erect his homestead.

I later learned that the words for the same activity were different because of the difference of the language spoken in the area. The language in the Pomeroon was different from that of Supenaam although the distance between the two areas was only about fifty miles as the bird flies. And to add to this, I later learned that there was regular trade between the areas. What was surprising, however, was that more people of the Pomeroon might have known of Kayap than people outside of Supenaam knew of Mashamuni. Perhaps this had to do with the greater degree of communication among the people of Pomeroon, with outsiders, than those of Supenaam.

Matriman

I became so enthused with this sort of activity, that, during one August holidays I travelled one hundred miles up the Mahaicony River. My second son and I were guests of the Headmaster of the St. Cuthbert's Mission on the Mahaica River, (a batch-mate from The Government Training College), when we were invited to the Mahaicony Mission. This seemed a great distance; but what we did not know was that it was closer than we thought. A journey about an hour in the tray of a tractor-and-trailer soon had us sipping yeast-tonic with some of our acquaintances.

This time, through the Head Master, we were invited to a "Matriman." I had had an idea to what kind of celebration we had been invited to, so this time the occasion was not a surprise. I surmised that the difference in sound might be due to a mispronunciation or a slight quirk in linguistic dialect. The word did not seem to belong to a different language.

Speeches and the ceremony had been finished before our arrival, so having been introduced to the Principals we joined wholeheartedly in the fun. I stared circulating among the local inhabitants and soon we were invited in a private home to share in their comforts. After a very comfortable night and a hearty breakfast, we stayed with a logger for two days (with himself and his men), and joined one forenoon in a "surum" gathering. This was the gathering of the very delicious maggot of the "tocuma" beetle, which was a great delicacy among the natives. Three weeks before they had cut down two ite trees and cut two "vees" just below the fronds and left them for the beetles to lay their eggs. The eggs hatched and the tiny pupa started eating the tender heart section of the ite and growing rapidly. After about three weeks or there-about the pupae are about an inch and a quarter long and packed with nutritious fat, ready to grow into a chrysalis, or harvested to be fried and eaten, or consumed raw. I prefer the creatures un-cooked.

(Above: the 'maggots' of the "tocuma" beetle. Source: www.stcuthbertsvillage.wordpress.org)

My son and I were offered passage out on a motorboat out to the Coast. We took advantage of this opportunity and returned to our home with indelibly entrenched experiences to our credit.

So this was another version of Kayap!

Manore

Years later when my employment took me to the North Savannahs of the Rupununi, I was taken by the Co-operative Officer to a Manore in the foothills of the picturesque Kanuku Mountains. After the ceremony and after some parakari imbibition, I wandered outside and sat alone on a log. I propped my back against a stump, closed my eyes and relived my Supenaam experience. I soliloquized that this is a concept conceived by people who really cared about one another. This type of activity spanned the length and breadth of the entire country and is an integral way of life among the indigenous people. Why, I wondered that such a laudable idea did not flower and fructify and bear results and become a way of life among ALL Guyanese.

It was this idea of lofty ideals and historical validity that the then government of Guyana chose as the rallying call for celebration at the anniversary of Guyana becoming a Republic. Guyana was granted independence from Britain on May 26,1966. In 1970 the date was set to celebrate it on the 23rd. February.

Guyana was granted independence from Britain in May 1966 under the Peoples' National Congress as the major party in a coalition government with the UF. Four years after Guyana was accorded Republican status in 1970. When the date was set to celebrate this on 23rd. Feb., rumor was rife that this date was chosen because it was around the time that was the birthday of the soon-to-be ruler, LFS Burnham. The PNC sought to validate the date by referring to the 1763 Slave Rebellion of Cuffy.

Since Independence there has been virtual stagnation in development in that little has changed under successive governments. As things seem to be going, without forward looking and progressive leaders, there is not even reasonable co-operation among members elected to run the country. It appears that the leaders have lost their reason and are intended on holding on to positions of power rather than enacting legislation for the benefit of all. Party "paramountcy" seems to be the pattern. In a situation like this it does not seem that there is much hope for a secure future, especially for marginalized groups.

This change was subtle, and hence was more destructive and dangerous. This bred widespread apathy and complacency. Hence only some noticed this downward spiral of the quality of life.

Many chose to vote with their feet, especially since America made it easier to obtain visas, especially among skilled people, thus encouraging producers in their prime to migrate.

It now has come to where extreme persuasion had to be used for people to celebrate the occasion. In some instances coercive means had to be used to get crowds to participate in the Annual Mashramani Celebrations. Renting buses and bussing crowds to various celebrations became the means to put up a facade for the press and pictures for international consumption.

Mashramani

The Government of the day has anglicized the word and regularized the use of the word as Mash-ra-mani. Although it still carries a mispronunciation to me, I have to come to accept it as the authentic word, since the spirit and the deed outweigh any sound of the word.

Over the years, less and less spontaneous participation became the order of the day, and it is now felt that it was a "derisory attempt to foster the concept, which was not, and has not been, wholly accepted by Guyanese". This non-acceptance was not because of the principle of Mashramani, but rather it was because of the dictatorial way these celebrations were foisted on the populace.

Recently I read in one of the local newspapers that the word "Co-operative" and "Socialist" will be expurgated from the Constitution of Guyana, since the country is neither "co-operative" nor "socialist." The country might have diverted from the socialist path, but can it divert from the laudable ideas and ideals of co-operation? The co-operation in Mashramani is the hallmark of/for development. It was conceived at the very grass-roots level and should be at the forefront of our development thrust which will make us prosper in the 21st. century. The concept and practice of Mashramani must live on, guiding our hearts and minds and informing our action. The Constitution must find a place for it, if not the word, then the concept. There is no other action or activity that fosters solidarity among individuals than working together for the common purpose.

The concept and spirit of Mashramani is a primary, if not a primal, effort of man in any society. And this should be more so among Third World societies, which can use all the dynamic forces to enable them to catch up with world development.

Things have changed in Guyana for the better, (so I have heard); therefore, from henceforth, as we participate in the ceremony of Mashramani, may it inspire Guyanese of all ilk to rise above partisan and race politics. Let us ignore those who would seek to divide us, or those who would sow the seed of prejudice and discontent, inequality and injustice among us. May Mashramani always remain golden in our memories, and may it see us through all our problems.

Long may Mashramani, Kayap, Matriman and Manore live!

****

A Mashramani Story

The Chief stood at the head of his people on the brow of the hill and looked upon the acres and acres of newly burnt fields that the entire tribe has worked on so hard to clear over an extended period of time - and thought... *"Three decades the tribe has fought against hostile forces since the near fatal rout by the hostile tribe that all but slaughtered the last few men. The decimated tribe constantly fought the hostile elements, scarcity of resources and amenities and bit by bit building the tribe and moving from spot to spot not only to escape man's hostilities but those imposed by natural forces."*

The Chief reminisced on the frustration he and his tribe encountered at every turn. Now for the second season in succession it seemed that the tribe has finally achieved a degree of stability with the help from an adjoining tribe; success seemed assured.

These thoughts raced through the head of the Chief as if a whirlwind had been passing and brought fresh hope to his tired mind and body. He had a premonition that from now onwards success will be assured and his people will continue to prosper in a stable and sustained fashion. The Chief felt good. As he gazed at the gentle slope that was the Hillside, he saw once again with his inner eyes as if in a titillating comatose manner that always soothed his mind and kept him in a euphoric state, he saw the land blooming like the Biblical Garden Of Eden with every fruit and flower that the mind of man can imagine. He saw cherubic children frolicking in flowered paths without a care on their visages, while the adults nonchalantly idled, watching their off-springs as they reveled in the slanting rays of the afternoon sunlight.

"The Garden of Eden," the Chief silently rolled the phrase on his tongue and thought, "Isn't the whole world meant to be a Garden of

Eden for the benefit of Man? Man's fall from grace because of disobedience has caused all his future travails. This thought shocked him out of his reverie and brought him to sudden realization.

There is yet hope he silently intoned. His tribe will, with the help of Manitou, transform this hillside to the materialization of his dreams. Is this not the self-same land that has yielded its abundance in times past? This is the same land that grew the abundance of fruits and vegetables in every corner that have nourished sons and daughters that have made history? It will do it again. Of this I am certain. The Chief closed his eyes once more and in his vision he saw the corn sprouting, the pumpkins running, the eddoes and cassava swelling fat in the soil, while sugar cane, papaws and melons decorate the sweeping landscape.

In the rivulets he saw sun fish and colorful luknanis, predatory houri and gourami lurking on the sidelines to seize any unwary minnow, while brilliant humming birds like gems flitting silently among the exotic orchids, and yellow and red mangoes tastefully contrasted with the huge bunches of green plantains and bananas that make a fitting green lacy fringe against the vertical wall of the uncut forest that stood like a tapestry setting off the scene in nothing less than regal splendor. The Chief reluctantly awoke from his reverie and turned his back towards the burnt fields and calmly addressed all who were present.

He leaned on his digging stick and, with all the strength he could summon, commenced to address them. He had come prepared with an adequate amount of seeds in his pouch: "Former people of the Highlands", he paused and looked around at all of them, "with these seeds that I have laboriously saved over a long time you will plant this the land that I have finally brought you to. Do it with the outmost love. Remember from love cometh love. If you do as I advise, your labor will reward you richly. On this land lies your destiny. Knowing this now, you can safely plan for your future and the future of your children and your children's children. This land is not completely won, but must be worked to produce. You may never be always successful, but remember what our people have gone through. There must always be the dream that bad weather does not occur every year, but has a degree of reliable predictability. Knowing this you can plan for the future. You must be vigilant and not only guard against slugs, snails and nematodes, that infest this your future, but also guard against the predators and ne'er do wells who will seek to pillage and destroy the fruits of your labor. I have the fervent belief that one and all of you are ably capable to carry out this mandate for the future of the tribe. You have the capability, and the land has the potential. What is there to stop you? I have brought you to your Eden and I am tired; but, remember this last advice and practice it always. Wherever you have found one seed, let there be two. If perchance a brother does you a kind deed, do him two, not because you are repaying, but because good is good to do. And if perchance he slaps your cheek, turn and offer the other one - with a smile". So spoke the Chief on "The Hillside of His Dreams" to his people.

He slowly straightened his bent body that was draped on his digging-stick and rose tall and stately and slowly ambled to his hut. But, even as he was doing so, he felt an emotional lump in his throat and a stabbing and annoying pain in his ribs.

The emotional pain he can well understand, but the other puzzled him. In all his days with and among his people and even with others who demanded that he do more, he could not remember such excruciating pain. In front of him appeared the visage of his late wife. He closed his eyes at this surreal vision. Perhaps it was a missed meal, or when he slid on that cut log climbing up to the brow of the hill; or is the vision of a better tomorrow that caused such pain? How could he think that such frivolous and mundane things can stop him, could stop "The Hillside of his Dreams!"

The Chief ambled to his hammock and raised his vision and looked to the future, a blazing canvas of colors in his mind. As the vision of the future became more intense so did the pain. It did not now nag but stabbed with increasing intensity then slowly morphed into a pernicious ache. He did not flinch nor complain when the icy hand of his wife gently smoothed his brow. A smile crossed his face as he cleared his throat and mumbled painlessly to his companion, "Everything will be all Right".

There never was seen before - maybe never since the days of the Pied Piper - such an out-pouring of grief and sadness at the demise of the Chief. You know what? The termites came out of the woodwork with long faces of disbelief, the fishes in the water cried so loudly that the vibration on the green fruits above caused them to fall off their branches. The lamb and the tiger walked together and did not bother to bother one another. Even the slugs and snails refused to destroy the ground crops and unashamedly shared in the common grief. And erstwhile enemies, when they heard of his demise wept openly, and reluctantly admitted that in their lifetime no greater one ever lived.

Today the concept of the cut, cleared and burnt field lives on. This concept and practice is embedded in the psyche of the people. It is a concept that is practically utilitarian and has proven itself again and again not only during crises but during good times also. It is by and large the only tried and tested method to get things done with the involvement of everyone. Guyana today needs, as the Chief advocated, the involvement of all. One of our great sons Martin Carter admonished that, "All are involved - all are consumed".

As we celebrate Mashramani ------ may we keep alive the Dreams of the Chief, and may----------- I reiterate as I did ------ that from this year and every other year as we participate in the Ceremony of Mashramani, may it inspire Guyanese and others of all ilk and persuasion to rise above partisan and race politics. Let us ignore those who would seek to divide us, or those who would sow the seeds of prejudice and discord, discontent and injustice. May Mashramani always remain golden in our memories and may it see us through all our dreams. This is The Way. The way not only to make the Dream on the Hillside come true but also to propel progress forward, the way of self-reliance and self-sufficiency.

45

(Above: Guyanese (Amerindians) in costume for Mashramani: Source: www.guyanatimesinternational.com)

****

Kanaima, The Enigma: *Myth or Reality*

In any village a "Kanaima" may dwell as an ordinary person among the rest of the populace unknown to anyone. Kanaima is known chiefly by what he does and his modus operandi. Although it is said that Kanaima is a man, it is not known for certain. But, basically, someone is attacked by Kanaima in reprisal for some wrong committed on some other person. Sometimes the wrong may even be perceived.

Once Kanaima has visited a person, he dies a slow painful and excruciating death.

Legend has it that the mode of operation of the Kanaima is as follows: another wrongs a person so sorely that he suffers loss to life or property, or both. The wronged party or a confidante or relative will threaten to put Kanaima on the perpetrator. The mere threats may scare the living daylights out of the person, or may be enough to cause the return of the stolen article, or for reconciliation in material of psychological terms, in which case the threat is not carried out. However, if this is not done, the help of Kanaima is sought.

Since no one ever knows who he is, or has ever seen him, this seems an impossible undertaking. But this is not so. The aggrieved party let it be known how much he will pay in food or other commodities if he is avenged. These will be left in a secluded part in the forest and it will be generally made known, except for the exact location. Superstition is so rife among the natives that everyone knows that to interfere with the price of Kanaima is strict taboo and hence none will ever interfere if he ever suddenly comes upon the stash.

The hirer will visit the cache to see if it is accepted. If it is not enough, a sign will be left that the price is not commensurate with the gravity of the crime. The aggrieved party will then add more to the store until Kanaima will secretly take the cache away. The aggrieved party now awaits results.

Somehow or the other Kanaima knows the aggrieved party, and now commences to study every move and habit of the wrong doer, and awaits the opportunity to catch him alone - this, regardless of how long it takes. The intended victim will now be secretly waylaid. Kanaima will stun the perpetrator as soon as he catches him alone with a deft blow to his anatomy that will leave no visible mark. This he does with a specially made purple-heart club.

If the victim is so stunned and rendered unconscious, then Kanaima will somehow arouse him into consciousness. It is imperative that the person is conscious so that he must know that he is paying for his misdeeds, or in the next life he will be prone to repeat the same mistakes again.

As soon as this state occurs, Kanaima sets to work on the victim. He first uses a secret method known only to him to get the victim's intestine to protrude so much that he can now tie the intestine into knots or lace it with poisonous spikes from his bag and pierce the tongue with a few, leaving the spikes embedded. By this time the victim becomes unconscious. His tongue gets so swollen partially from the poison in the greenheart spikes and partially from the wounds, that his mouth is now completely filled with his tongue. This renders him completely speechless by the time he has regained consciousness and staggers back to the village.

The victim's bodily functions now cease. He cannot eat nor speak because his body is being slowly paralyzed as the poison creeps to his more vital organs. The entire village will now know that he has been paid a visit by Kanaima and is paying the ultimate price for some misdeed. The family and the village know that there is no cure and they cannot find out who Kanaima is. (It must be known that there was no method of writing for communication then among the natives of the savannah during this period). The victim, apart from being unable to eat, cannot also drink. He suffers a slow dehydration as he profusely sweats his body away. As soon as the perspiration stops, his body starts to swell. He dies in his hammock and is wrapped in it and is buried in the earthen floor. The hut is burnt over his grave.

Many tales of Kanaima are told throughout the length and breadth of Guyana among all the Amerindian tribes. It is well known that the tribes of the North West District and the forested regions (who island hopped and inhabit the Coastal and near-by regions of The Sand and Clay Belt) are well aware of Kanaima as are the migrants from the Amazon. While some claim that the Kanaima story points to a common ancestry, the lore might well have been spread by the traders among these people eons ago. It is well documented that there was brisk trade between the inhabitants of the savannahs and inhabitants who lived on the Orinoco delta and further afield. However, whether or not Kanaima exists, or is a figment of the imagination, it has served to modify the lives of all the native peoples and served as a barometer of control of social behavior.

Even today, with the advent of Christianity and especially Roman Catholicism, that most if not all of the native hunters do not go into the forest to hunt unaccompanied. They at least go in pairs, and if there is not a male to accompany a hunter, he may even take his wife along.

Nestled in the foothills of the South Savannah is, to my mind, the most picturesque village in all the hinterland. Sand Creek, in the late afternoon, is a picture perfect canvas of what constitutes an ideal photograph, fit to adorn the cover of the best Nature Magazine.

Nerso lived in a benab near the forest that was cut off abruptly where the mountain ended and the flat savannah begun. On this peripheral location it was hard to determine whenever he was

(Above: two 'benabs' in the Rupununi. Photo Credit: Jennifer Wishart, Georgetown, Guyana)

home or not. Nevertheless he never missed any of the communal activities of the village, neither activities that required manual labor, nor those communal meetings that are required for the effective running of the village. He had ample reasons not to. As far as anyone knows, he was never married, but he had a daughter who kept his benab spick and span, who cooked and washed and did all in her power to maintain a home as if a mother was present.

When, sometime ago Nerso migrated from the village of Caracarai, from over the border in Brazil, as he alleged to be his former home, he chose Sand Creek as his new village of residence. At this time his daughter Mika was only three years old and needed a mother. As he lodged in the guest hut, he was helped by the village touchau to choose a spot nearest to the forest on the periphery to locate the benab that he wanted to build.

Having chosen the spot, he now commenced to make adobe bricks, which he stocked in piles as soon as they were dry enough.

As his daughter played with the village children, he went to the creek, climbed the ite-palm trees, cut enough leaves for thatch and laboriously lugged them to his adobe pile. The next week he went to the adjoining forest and cut and peeled enough frame-wood for the roof. He next hauled all this to the location.

One difficulty now arose. Since he was without a wife to plan with, her friends and other helpers to plan and execute a Manore, (the communal activity that will ensure the easy erection of the benab), the erection of his home seemed onerous. However when he put the problem to the village Chief, he was promised much help, seeing that Nerso has done so much on his own.

The Chief called his young warriors together who agreed to accompany Nerso into the mountains to hunt meat for the Manore. In the meanwhile the Chief's wife prepared a huge plastic barrel of parakari while some young men erected tables and benches for the coming occasion. On the third day the hunters returned with four half-smoked quarters of kamma and the smoked carcasses of two wild boars.

Early the next morning, as the women prepared the huge pots of food, the men expertly fixed, pasted and daubed smooth the four adobe walls, leaving one doorway and three windows at the direction of Nerso. The rafters for the roof were soon in place and these were interspersed with manicole strips on which the ite fronds were attached as neatly thatched as can be imagined and as watertight as can be.

By three o'clock in the afternoon, having cleanly swept the area, Nerso and Mika moved their scant belongings into their newly constructed benab. They slung their hammocks and hung their warashis on pegs embedded in the walls for them.

The entire village gathered around and assembled to hear the Chief laud their successful effort and the Peiman give his benediction. The men, freshly washed after their hard work, with fresh shirts and neatly oiled hair, faced the women in their bright floral dresses. After the ceremonial and initial drinking of the parakari started, individuals produced a guitar, a wooden drum, two shak-shaks and a mouth organ and a tambourine and the merriment started. Quickly, some lively and spirited gyrations took place, but this soon died down and made way for more sober dancing.

I want to note at this point that the rhythms orchestrated among these uninhibited people have to be experienced to be appreciated. With the setting rays of the sun scattered among the sparse stunted trees casting streaks of gold in the background, the uninhibited and primitive music emanating from the brightly dressed performers in this otherwise tranquil setting transports the individual in throes of silent ecstasy.

A wrestling match late in the afternoon left two young men sprawled on the stubble and only the crisp night air descending from the mountain revived them when they singly sidled to their own benabs.

Years passed quickly. Mika grew up into a very pretty maiden of fifteen. Rains came and seasons passed. Life went on peacefully. But when all seemed right, certain inexplicable occurrences started to happen, some of them good, some of them not so good.

Imagine one hot and sultry mid-day, when everyone was supposed to be having their siesta, a jaguar chased a kamma from the mountains straight into the village. The commotion woke up the torpid men who, with lances and bows and arrows, bravely surrounded the animals in the vicinity of Nerso's benab.

(Above: jaguar of Guyana. Source: www.adventureguians.com)

They dispatched the kamma as the sagacious jaguar slithered straight through the open door of Nerso's hut. Thinking that Nerso was in his field, (having not seen him since early morning), they left the kamma and went and fetched dry ite fronds and some metallic sheets to make noise and, perchance, chase out the dangerous animal from Nerso's hut, and maybe kill it to sell the dried pelt in Brazil where it would fetch a fair price.

The men surrounded the benab, all but the side that had the door, so as to give the beast a chance to run out and present a clear shot. Some cautiously approached the three openings that served as windows with lighted brands of ite fronds in their hands over their heads. Another started to make such a din on the metal sheets they had, they could have awakened the dead as it were. At about a hundred feet away, others positioned themselves behind makeshift shelters, armed with lances and clubs and bows and arrows.

As soon as the din started, whom do you think poked his head through the window gap with his hands over his brows? Nerso calmly enquired what the fracas was about. If he had not shouted at the top of his lungs, the men might have taken his yellow visage for that of the jaguar; and who knows what they would have done? They were so surprised that the noise stopped abruptly. The men with the fire dropped their brands and frightenly joined the others peering into the benab . The other men who were stationed behind the various shelters, having heard the din stop, wanted to ascertain the cause. No one was more surprised than they were as they saw the others come around to the door to greet the owner as he strode into the sunshine with a perplexed grin on his normally stoic face.

Everyone was awe-struck that it took some time to explain to Nerso his/her strange behavior. He evinced no surprise but went to the carcass of the kamma, touched the tough hide with his finger and then the finger to his forehead. Not even a smile of surprise or any facial movement marred the thin compressed lips as he gazed around at his neighbors. The men retired to the shade of a cashew tree to discuss the noonday happening. His daughter, Mika, now appeared at the entrance to the door blinking her eyes to shade them from the slanting rays of the sun.

In the bright rays of the afternoon sun, the men quartered the carcass of the kamma and lugged the parts to the communal square for the women to further dress, prior to parceling out to the different households.

Since three windows were covered with stiffly stretched cotton blinds, the men wanted to know how the jaguar escaped without disturbing Nerso or Mika or even knocking the blinds from their fastenings.

Of course Nerso doubted if any jaguar will drive its prey towards human habitation. Both of these creatures were normally nocturnal he reminded them. The kamma must have strayed down from the mountains in search of water. He asked the villagers to dismiss the jaguar as some figment of their imagination. Of course a parakari party ended the day with the men discussing the recent happening until all felt sleepy and each retired to their respective homes.

The second strange thing that happened was on the day Nerso led his four companions to an allegedly overfished creek not far from the village. He instructed his companions to secrete themselves at the fork of the creek as he went some distance upstream. He told his companions that when they heard a long high-pitched whistle they must make all haste to approach him, making as much noise as possible as they came near.

They hid themselves near the water on the bank of the creek. The water suddenly started to get cloudy and then very silted with leaves, sand and other debris passing down in more extravagant profusion. They were contemplating this strange phenomenon when, as if from among them, arose an eerie whistle, so clear and apparently near, as temporarily to paralyze them with awe and root them to their spot of hiding. But they suddenly remembered Nerso's instruction and, as if waking from their reverie, they got up as one and started making as much noise as their lungs will allow them.

They carefully made their way among the tacoubas and other deadfall and found no time to cogitate on the eerie whistle. However, before anyone could voice a thought, there appeared in front of them, their friend Nerso. He silently beaconed that they follow. After a little distance they all looked in the direction where his index finger was pointing. They were flabbergasted when they beheld between the great buttresses of a mora tree, a big pile of fishes, haimara and pacu, kuti and dari, sunfish and lukanani, and many others not seen around in a long time. Each fish had a neat bite behind its head above each eye. Most appeared to be dead but a few showed signs of life by weakly flapping their tails and panting with opening and closing their gill-slits.

Each person looked at the other with amazement as if the fish presented a supernatural spectacle. Nerso ordered each man to cut fronds from a nearby small ite tree and to plait darwans. This was soon complied with and each filled his handled containers. When all the fish was accounted for they each slung two of these baskets around their shoulders and made their way home. The females gutted, scaled, washed and drained the fish after which the Chief allocated each household their portion.

One sleepy afternoon a group of hunters were returning with some scanty booty when they encountered Nerso on a little trodden path in the forest shaving pieces of green-heart chips into spikes four-inches long, with a point at only one end. When they looked at him, he explained that he was making fishhooks. The hunters were a little leery of this explanation since it was given unasked and fishhooks that long cannot be used in any nearby streams. And besides, fishhooks had point on both sides. These observations, coupled with the agitated demeanor and an eye in which a tic was pulling at the corners, caused the hunters to reinforce the suspicion that the spikes were not meant to be fishhooks. Simultaneously the men espied Nerso's warashi, having sprouting from the sides, the flaccid leaves of certain herbs well known for their toxic qualities.

The new moon before, when Nerso had returned tired from his farm in the early afternoon and when the sun was dipping towards the horizon, he ducked his head to enter the door-way. As he was halfway through, from the dark interior came a rustle, and then a beam of faint light appeared to flash from the dim aperture that served as the window. Nerso knew that the blind was securely anchored at the four corners with stakes securely anchoring them to the hard adobe.

Mika, the daughter, who was now over fifteen, and had pleaded a temperature in the morning, did not accompany her father to the farm that day. She now appeared sound asleep in her hammock that was slung from two rafters from the far side from the door. However, as her father's eyes became accustomed to the pale light of the interior, he thought that he detected that the hammock was swinging ever so slightly.

As Nerso hung up his warashi on a peg, put up his bow and arrows and leaned his machete in a corner, he felt an inexplicable uneasiness. He went to the window and examined the fastenings. The two pegs that fastened the blind at the bottom were missing. This confirmed his suspicions that someone had been in the benab and escaped through the now unsecured blind. To reinforce these suspicions, as he bent down to search for the pegs, his fingers closed on an ornamental headband worn by some young men in the tribe. He found the pegs and secured the corners of the blind a new, hiding the headband in his pocket to examine it at his leisure, later.

Mika "woke" up and greeted her father then prepared his dinner. As was customary, her father ate in silence, washed his hands after some small talk and wended his way to the hunting hut where all the hunters will be discussing their day's exploits and their coming plans for the weekend hunting trip in the mountains.

As he left, he took out the headband and examined it. He could not ascertain to whom it belonged so he carefully put the tiny center bead between his two incisors and pressed with all his might. The miniature white glass bauble cracked in two and left its kurawa moorings. When the father returned from the meeting, he threw the headband under the window where he had found it and retired to his hammock.

The next time when the elders returned from their hunting expedition in the forests, it was already evening. After making plans for the next day, Nerso left the meeting hut and went home. He went to the spot where he had thrown the headband. It was gone.

During the next week he nonchalantly examined the headbands from every young man he encountered. Great was his surprise when he finally espied the marked headband adorning the forehead of the village wastrel, a youth known for his adroit ability to evade all physical exertion. Nerso felt let down by his only daughter's behavior. Not only that such behavior cuts across the mores of the tribe, but also to all a father holds dear for a beloved daughter, an only child. The gall rose in his throat as he recalled sadly why he left his beloved home in Caracarai so many moons ago.

Having decided on his future course of action, Nerso shadowed the young man until his every movement and behavior formed an integral part of his memory. One morning as the youth left the village to raid some fish traps in an adjoining settlement some distance away, Nerso followed him and waylaid him on a bend in the path as he was returning with his ill-gotten booty.

A dull thud to a secret part of his anatomy laid the young man low. Nerso quickly took from his sack the various paraphernalia. He looked at the victim's eyes to make sure that he was conscious. He next laced some of the spikes through the lad's tongue and pushed it back into his mouth. His tongue swelled almost instantly to fill his mouth. Popping his vertebra in the middle, Nerso deftly pushed on the youngster's abdomen until his large intestine protruded out of his anus to some length. This he laced with the poisonous spikes and then reinserted them into the abdominal cavity. Nerso now left the semi-conscious youth near to the quake of stolen fish and made a hasty retreat.

When the hapless youth awoke in the twilight, he found that he could not talk or use his mouth for anything. The lower part of his abdomen was excruciatingly painful and swollen. He stumbled home and, by the end of the week, he was in the great benab in the sky among his ancestors.

Although the whole village knew that it was Kanaima that has done him in, everyone felt that it was just cause for stealing, for it was soon discovered that the person who had been robbing the fish traps had been the youth.

Nerso kept a close look on his daughter's demeanor and paid keen attention to all of her behavioral idiosyncrasies. However he learned very little from her usual stoicism.

On one of the longest speeches he would ever make to his daughter, one afternoon after dinner, in the semi-darkness of the benab, Nerso finally got his daughter's attention.

"My kulasali," (= thrush), "a father knows his daughter's heart. Although you think that it is the dry season of your life, and all your crops are destroyed, keep this advice I am giving you for always. You cannot remember your dear mother. Maybe this is best. You only know life with me. Hear me well. After every drought, there is bound to come rain. After the darkest night there will be sunlight; even behind the darkest cloud there is sunlight. Do you understand what I am hinting at, my bird? Daddy knows what is best for his child".

"I hear you, my father, and I understand, although my heart is heavy. Fathers know best," Mika said resignedly, and sadly retired to the dark interior of her hammock clutching a headband with the center bead missing.

(Above: modern young Amerindian woman: Source: www.stabroeknews.com)

****

THE LEGENDS

The Final Great Meeting

The great Chief of Arewak was awaiting the great moment, two moons hence, with the greatest anticipation. It was eons ago that they left their homes in Pura and journeyed into the rising sun. The first great migration into the setting sun was a faint memory among the storytellers of the tribe.

Young and old alike revered the repositories of the tribal culture, The Wise Ones. No one can ever remember not having one among themselves in every great household. In the days long gone by, when the earth was young it was a regular ritual for all and sundry to gather around the fire and listen to the Wise Ones recall the great sagas of the people. Everyone was required to listen without the slightest interruption and indicate by an appropriate sound that he was keenly listening and following the trend of the story.

So tradition was handed down and never lost. The Wise Ones must have embellished some deeds from time to time, but the traditional lore, the history and the basic facts were handed down from father to son among the Chosen Ones and so remained intact down the ages.

The First Migration it must be recalled occurred when rivalry broke out between the two great houses of the Inca. Word had come from the North that a great sage had seen in his dream that the Rulers of the Sky will arrive in the not too distant future and create havoc among the People.

While some described this as old wives tales, some firmly believed in the omens of the future as foretold by the Wise Ones. They recalled how, not so long ago, that it was impossible to see in the heads of people. Now the Wise Ones in their infirmaries were routinely cutting into the heads of sick people to remove tumors and treat schizophrenia.

They also recalled that once, tribute to the Great Inca could have been any amount, but today the Collectors were able to keep meticulous records of the tributes of everyone on some mysterious strings. The Wise Ones foretold even the Great Migration. Has it not come to pass that dissention in the two families has come to pass as foretold? Had they not taken provisions and sailed into the setting sun never to be seen or heard from again? The Wise Ones still drew vivid word pictures of how the entire family of a great house vanished into the setting sun on their balsa rafts as some mourning relatives looked on! There is still no agreement among the Elders whether the migrants were swallowed up by the Great Waters or had been mysteriously drawn up into the Heavens to reside forever with the Gods. They still, without fail, journey to the Great Mesa on the anniversary of the event to gaze into the setting sun and relive the moment. Some still see the rafts being wafted to Heaven, while others still swear that they see the Great Waters swallowing them up.

Today in this great hour of tribulation, Great Chief Kurawa sat on the ceremonial stool in the dimly lit recesses of the great house soliloquizing of how he must recall to his people, not this first migration, but the second great one that now has the People so scattered as chaff on the wind that used to sweep down from the mountains of Pura to the sea.

(Above: Amerindian communal 'benab'. Source: www.dpi.gov.gy)

Once he recalled that they were known as The People the Children of the Sun God. They worshipped the sun and lived by its rules. They even bathed the Great Inca with the sun-dust as the earthly representative of the One who sees all. Those were the days when they were like children, innocent and protected all around by God and man. The time when chuno and quinoa were abundant, and the weather was mild rather than hot.

According to the Great Grandfather of seventeen generations ago the Sages foretold the second migration when the so-called Children of the Sky invaded the territory. These invaders were strange people. Their eyes were blue and their skins were the color of paiche, the white-bellied fish they caught from the cold mountain-streams, and their hair was the color of dried grass.

They came into the peoples' homes as guests and remained to take over their wives and nubile daughters. What was most disturbing was that they brought with them strange diseases. These diseases, once caught, decimated the population. And as if this was not sufficient they chased the men out of their homes to search for the yellow sun dust for which they had an insatiable appetite.

The people were powerless to resist. The strangers' long broad swords and their mysterious fire-sticks kept them superior. Unknown to these invaders, they were to take back to their homelands a devastating sexual disease unknown to them then, but to which the Children of the Sun were quite immune having contracted and developed immunity to it eons ago. Eating infected llama meat had initially caused them to contract the disease.

Then, rather than die under the pressure of the new comers, secret meetings were held in the fields in the evenings, and it was agreed that the entire village would move out under the cover of darkness during the first dark phase of the next new moon.

Secret preparations were made. Since there was no supervision in the fields the men secretly cached essentials for many days' flight that lay ahead, along trails in the mountains unknown to the strangers.

There was a great feast to celebrate the darkest night of the year. This, according to tradition and the counting of the High Priests, occurred once every twenty-five years during the month of April. There was great revelry. The people were overtly nice to the visitors. They plied the invaders with all the drinks they wanted. Unknown to them the drinks were laced with a secret narcotic obtained from the adjacent forest. The guests did not disappoint the hosts. They copiously imbibed of the mild liquor. Before long, the satiated participants staggered to their quarters or fell where they were to sleep off the mild yet potent intoxicant.

The Second Migration started. By midnight, the entire native population was far into the mountains, 'over the bump', and down the other side taking a little known trail that led into the headwaters of a secret stream that would eventually lead them into the Great Maranon.

Great hardships did they endure, especially the women and children, during the first weeks. Used as they were to the climate of the leeward side of the mountains, they were ill prepared for the drenching downpours of rain that characterized these windward slopes. There will be piercing sunlight one moment penetrating the verdant forests, and the next moment torrential downpours that bathed everything in humid yet debilitating freshness. One redeeming factor was that the showers were warm and provided respite from the copious perspiration that was the order of their swift and headlong flight to escape.

Their enemies? Having woken up late the next day from their drunken stupor, the invaders made a half-hearted attempt to follow, but soon returned in frustration, refusing to believe that their erstwhile providers had vanished without ceremony. They made other attempts under other leaders to follow, but they returned each time empty-handed being frustrated by the dank humidity to which they were so unaccustomed.

The People, like the First Migration, seemed to have vanished into thin air. Folklore has it today that they had been reunited with their ancestors that vanished West so long ago. There is still argument among the unschooled intelligentsia that East and West, and the rising and the setting sun is one; only the directions are different. Can't up be down and down be up? They asked. Suppose that the earth was round? It depends upon which part of the mountain you are on.

The migrants fled for many moons until they felt sure that pursuit was impossible. They adroitly avoided the head hunting tribes when possible. Their sheer numbers and the ferocity of the vanguards and out-flanking warriors kept strangers at bay and served to protect the weak and vulnerable.

After many adventures and the slight thinning of their numbers they eventually reached a confluence of the great Maranon.

The land was good to them. They settled and prospered. The abundance assured larger and healthier families. They lost all contact with the land they had left. Only their culture and vivid memories remained. They tried to maintain the strong family ties but ever the younger, the more robust tended to move along. They strayed from the ways of the old ones and readily mingled and mixed with outsiders and thus integrated with less civilized inhabitants.

Although they were a sociable and gregarious people, the tribal and familial ties proved weaker than appeared on the surface. This did not augur well for homogeneity and sorely worried the elders who never failed to discuss this anomaly around their tribal fires. At one of these councils, they came to the painful decision that moving farther east down The Mother of the Waters was their only hope of preserving a cultural order that has lasted them throughout the centuries.

This they presently embarked on and eventually reached the confluence with the Rio Negro. This ebon stream entered its waters into the more frigid Maranon. Being warmer than the larger river by receiving more tropical heat, the waters refused to mix until many miles downstream.

There were many tribal debates around the fires for many moons regarding the future course of action. After many arguments and debates, which soured their tranquil relations somewhat, the main body moved North and West up the Negro, while a small and adventurous body of mostly young people continued down the main Maranon.

The main tribe lived successfully along the banks of this bounteous river, ever cultivating the fertile and gentle slopes of the multitude of river valleys found along the way. One thing that was very consistent however was a constant movement ever forward, away from an unseen enemy.

Since the break at the parting of the waters, several smaller, mostly young families, left the main tribe to pursue their destiny in various directions from the main body of old and stable units. This happened over many years and over many generations until they reached the Region of the Great Llanos.

Some, remembering their mountains, moved east into the Acarai while the bulk of the population moved ever forward. From the Rupununi they traded wild rice and other delicacies for bows and arrows, and settled around Arewa. They eventually, over many moons, became the two great tribes of the Macushi and the Wapishana, while a restless set continued to the Imataka. Today, over two hundred years from the initial flight from the almost forgotten land of Pura, word reached their Chief Kurawa via regular trader from the Orinoco delta, that men with pale white skins, matted hair and beards were journeying up the great river known as the Desekebe, and at that very moment were at the mouth where it joins the Roopoonooni.

These traders were well known since contact was always maintained with the main body through them. From the Orinoco they traded wild rice and other delicacies for bows and arrows, and the valuable and potent curare used in hunting. Those in the Acarai also kept in contact with the main group.

The news of the White men awakened a deep, instinctive and feral fear, inactive and suppressed, but very much alive. After verifying this fact from dispatching some runners, Chief Kurawa kept counsel with the Elders of the now two great clans. They decided that it was the opportune time to summon all the tribes with whom contact can be made. A mass decision with popular support was needed if the People were to survive.

A date was named and runners were dispatched even to the remotest tribe. A great meeting was called for the next full moon. The time was ample for everyone to get to Arewa.

There was a frenzy of preparation as heads of household supervised the making of huge amounts of farine and tapioca. There were strict orders not to make any parakari since only sober heads were needed to make the best decisions. All the best hunters set out and eventually returned with great amounts of capy, (capybara), paca and deer almost daily. Fish was also caught in abundance. All was jerked and stored for the coming event. One set of men built a benab so large as to accommodate a thousand men, women and even entire families, with facilities enough to afford a modicum of privacy among participants too.

In a few days, the nearer tribes started to arrive from all points of the compass, and even from between those points as they journeyed to the meeting. As they arrived the Chief Kurawa greeted each personally, or a lesser personage of high rank as befitted the rank of the visitor.

At last, the last of the chiefs arrived. He was from the Northwest. It was his traders who carried the news of the White men to Chief Kurawa, and then back to their own chief. From that day onwards they maintained daily surreptitious watch on the strangers and reported the progress to their respective Chiefs.

Early on the day of the full moon, the great meeting began under the chairmanship of the great Kurawa. He, being the host, became the natural leader. It was his great-great-great-grandfather who sanctioned the break at the parting of the waters on the Great Maranon. This grandfather was the one who led the greater part of the tribe along and up the stream of ebon hues. Chief Kurawa's agenda required that each tribe offer up prayers to the various Dieties, Makanaima and Acarai, Aconcagua and Imataca and all the others, each according to his own fashion. They fervently offered up their supplications, asking the blessing, and seeking advice, help and clarity in their present deliberations.

This being done, he outlined their present situation after recounting their history from their initial flight from the land of their ancestors to their present situation. "I have convened this meeting," he concluded, "so that we may, as a people, discuss our plight, and come to a consensus regarding our future actions, not as diverse families, household or tribes, but as a Nation, as a People, as Children of the sun God". He paused a moment and seemed to be thinking deeply. Through his mind was passing the greatness of his ancestors, while in front of him, clear as day, was the strangulation of his People. Tears seeped from his tightly closed eyes, and as if with great pain he asked, "What has become of the nobility that illuminated the lives of the Ancestors?" He sat down with closed eyes as if expecting an answer, but none came from the utter silence that permeated the gathering, like the Kanuku fog in the Southeast background. A deep sob escaped as if from the inner recesses of his being.

As if by prior arrangement, each tribe, group and clan occupied the position in the Great Benab, as they would have as represented on a map of the landscape. A squat sedate Chief from the northwestern corner rose. Although there was hardly a sound, all eyes turned automatically in his direction. "I... we... have seen the bearded ones, they visited our village, ate of our food, asked about the direction and location of the mountain from which we got the yellow metal that made the ornament that adorned my wife's ears. Because of their demeanor, we answered that there was an abundance of the useless metal some day's travel up the stream. Before they left they took a dozen of our young men to man their canoes. We never saw our young men again." Some heads nodded in affirmation as if to say, "that is true".

After a respectable amount of silence, from the center, a tall gaudily dressed individual rose. He started by deliberately looking at the last speaker and began, "My brother was lucky. In my village in the Desekebe, these devils make periodic raids. They do not only carry off our men, but also our young women. A few of our men managed to escape and came back with terrible tales of the ways of the blue-eyes".

Tribe after tribe, clan after clan recounted horror stories of the strangers, of their strange habits, and of their intense desire to get their hand on the yellow metal. From every corner except the deep southeast can be heard murmurings of the wickedness, the ferocity, the strange ways, the brutalities and ill qualities of the strangers. But, over-riding all this, was the intense desire and greed for the yellow metal so useless, unlike food and drink or clothing, but used for mere adornment.

At last from the remotest South east corner of the benab arose Chief Pingohoto. He raised his right hand and there was utter silence. "We have never experienced the Whiteman except in our remote memories", he intoned, "But we have heard stories of him. I think that once he learns that our land has a lot of the yellow stuff, we will be in the greatest danger. From our deliberations, it seems that we are completely surrounded and hemmed in by these invaders. This means that we have nowhere else to run. It is my advice, if the Great Kurawa would permit that we break into mixed committees, discuss the situation thoroughly, offer solutions, and meet at the setting of the sun each day to report our findings."

Meanwhile runners constantly report the progress of the White men up the river. After three days and three days of deliberations when the waning of the moon was already discernible, a final decision was made at the Final General Council. This discussion continued far into the final night. The final decisions will never be known. This is a closely guarded secret, handed down to only chosen ones.

However, it was decided for the first time in their lives, that they will never again run. The way of life in the future with strangers will be one of reluctant accommodation; they will even keep their names secret and retain their language for use only among them-selves and learn all they can of the ways of the invaders.

There was immediate need not to leave an iota of trace of this meeting, so when night arrived, each tribe and household withdrew to a safe distance, and the Great Benab was set alight.

The White men saw the glow in the sky and believed, as was told them, that it was one of the savannah fires. When everything was reduced to mere ashes and was cold, each person took some of this ash, wrapped it in a little hide-pouch and took it with him. All the tribes have this sacred pouch onto this day. This serves as a memento for the renewal of the covenant of the Great Meeting at

Arewa.

By the evening of the next day there was not the slightest trace that the Greatest Meeting of the Children of the Sun God had ever taken place.

The Chief Kurawa had hardly retired to his hammock the following night when a runner awakened him with some strangers at his heels. In the compounded glow of the firelight at his back and the pale half-moon behind the strangers, he was greeted with an outstretched hand. "I am Im Thurn, Evarard ImThurn," the stranger said.

(Amerindian great 'benab' Guyana. Photo Credit www.peteoxford.com)

(This story was told to me while I was residing among some Wapishana friends. I was on a hunting trip to one of the various hunting areas in the headwaters of one of the creeks, the name of which I have now forgotten. We were all close together in shelters called powis-tails which consisted of a few turu leaves stuck in the ground to give shelter from the elements).

****

WHY the CAYAMBAY (Curatella Americana) IS PYROCLASTIC

Billions of years after The Big Bang, and after viscid volcanic action had ceased, and millions of years of erosion had made the earth fertile, giant plants and microscopic organisms populated the earth in richest profusion. All plants were edible before the advent of animals. Plants only developed their spines and spicules, their toxins and thorns, and their profuse propensity for poisons after lower animals started voraciously consuming them.

Legend has it that trees used to communicate with one another, and later, animals and plants used to communicate also. As time went by this communication was lost; first, between animals and plants, i.e. between herbivores and plants, and then between plants and plants. According to the degree of friendship or enmity, certain plants got away from the animals that ate them. Many of the plants palatable to terrestrial animals migrated to the swamps beyond their reach, while those harassed by aquatic creatures migrated to a terrestrial abode. Some, like the cactus, even migrated to lands uninhabitable, even to them, and adapted to an inhospitable environment.

Some succulents even migrated to underwater domains to hide their sugar and succulence from the enemies. On the other hand, some terrestrial animals, like the moose, were so hooked on certain tastes that they followed the plants down under the water and can still be seen even today ducking their heads and immersing themselves completely in the quest for their favorite cuisine.

Whenever this happened, because animals were more mobile, they were always to pursue their favorite fare. Plants pleaded and pleaded but to no avail after which they all decided that they will cease to talk with animals forever. Some plants like the pitcher plant and the Venus flytrap agreed among them-selves to retaliate in a different way. They started to eat dinosaurs, but when these died out they started to starve and became miniaturized in their stature and hence today must be content with eating small insects.

Every plant at this time bore no flowers, they were beautiful unto themselves. They bore neither fruits nor seeds but propagated themselves by spores. However, each plant was edible. After they withdrew their speech they defended themselves with various devices, but any humane ones decided that they will bear attractive, delicious and edible fruits which animals may eat and so leave the bearers alone.

And then humans came on the scene. Having a large brain, some of them readily understood that they were made of the same stuff of not only the animals, which they ate, but also the plants. After they understood they established a relationship with the plants that continued on to this day. Those plants that they ate, they cultivated, and those that were beautiful they cared for, and even took some of them to live in their homes. It is to those that humans talk. In some hallowed and silent instances, some even answer their hosts. This has even led to the study of the nervous system of plants. Some say that the nervous system of plants is rudimentary, but man's quest has proved that the transmission of neural messages operate under the same principles as the so-called higher animals.

Is it any wonder that ancient man asked a tree's permission before cutting it for utilitarian purposes? Don't some of them accord the same respect for the animals that they kill for their sustenance? Is it only among contemporary man that wanton destruction of both flora and fauna occurs at an unprecedented rate without leave? The ramifications of man's actions may have future dire consequences if this remains unchecked.

It was during this time when Earth was young, when all plants were palatable and had just exorcised consortium with animals, that there lived in the shadow of the Imataka Mountains, near the llanos of Venezuela, a stately bloom. This tree was so versatile that it bore fruits during the rains and also during the dry season. This tree also bore many different kinds of fruits that gave sustenance to man and beast alike.

The leaves were big, bright shiny laminas that could shade anyone from the rain and sun alike. The flowers it bore were displayed in large inflorescences that reflected the rain and sun alike in dozens of iridescent hues to delight both the eyes and inner sensibilities of the beholder. The bark of this wondrous tree could have been used in a variety of ways, from the most soothing poultices for acne, to medicines for exterminating worms. The fiber of the bark was used to make the finest cloth. The wood of this tree also forms the mortar-piece from which the earliest inhabitants started fire. When the roots were exposed they displayed exquisite contours to delight the eye and heart of the most fastidious artist. The canopy was so packed with verdant foliage as to offer complete shelter from the rays of torrid Sol. Man and beast lived in its shade and fed on its luscious fruits while exotic birds with all the hues of creation flitted among its branches.

In the entire world only this one small area had trees like these. There was a fair amount of these trees but the favorite among them was the one that was perched on the side of a cool stream that issued from a crevice of the sandstone mesa some ten miles away. This was the largest tree and seemed to be the mother of all the others. The area was pristine and picture-perfect, and served as the meeting place for all animals, and the trysting place for lovers.

This area of primordial trees of manna lay betwixt the land of the Macushi and that of the Patamona. So it was not strange for these two warring clans to be feasting and frolicking under adjacent trees or among trees that were in close proximity howbeit on opposite sides of the shallow stream.

Since, among all beings, mealtime was not yet set by their biological clocks, at any time man and beasts could have been found feasting themselves of the delicious and varied bounty.

It was in the soft grass on a mat of hay under one of the trees that the Patamona considered their private property, (being nearer to their domain than that of the Macushi), that Shea found the sleeping and still tired Kako wrapped in the fetal position, dead to all the world, it seemed. Immediately Kako sprung up, seized his bow and put an arrow to its string. Seeing it was a beautiful girl, (fairer than all his savannah kinsmen), he stayed his hand. At this instant Shea raised her right hand palm facing forward in the universal gesture of peace. Their eyes met and their gazes locked in a primordial act of understanding, older than the sandstone escarpment that was filtering the early sunlight between its vertical outlines. For a long moment both stood thus, each in a turmoil of emotion that was understandable yet belying the understanding.

At that very moment as the seeds of love were watered in the hearts of these two young people, two white doves and a golden cock-of-the-rock arose from the ground in serene majesty towards the pinnacle of the tree. This omen of peace and opportunity seemed to awaken in the breast of both of them the torrid history of their tribes. Both now moistened their dry lips and throats and retreated backwards from each other, their eyes still locked in a gaze that changed from shock to surprise, from surprise to a primeval recognition of an emotion older than time itself.

Kako returned to his household and led them to the splendid tree on his side of the river, while Shea and her people feasted off the bounty of the tree on the other side.

Each evening while the sides eyed each other from their side with hostile equanimity, the two silent lovers dangled their feet in the soothing waters and locked their gazes lovingly.

A few days later Kako had surreptitiously discovered the place where Shea slept during the night. He silently forded the stream and crept in her direction. As if by prearrangement, Shea silently rose from her bed of reeds, looked furtively towards her sleeping companions, and silently wended her way towards the river. Prostrate, Kako listened to the swish of the feet in the tall grass. At first he thought that it was some wild beast that made the sound, but his trained ear at once recognized a bipedal gait. He cautiously elevated his sight and soon the silhouette of the one he sought appeared.

As he identified the shadowy outline, he clicked the tune of the quadrille, (a diurnal musical wren peculiar only to this part of the South American Continent). Shea was taken aback at first, since on three previous nights, her expectations never paid off. For the first time it appeared that her prayers were answered. She cautiously replied in like fashion. Kako rose and, with outstretched arms, melted silently into his loving embrace. No word was said as they made their way to the most luxuriant tree of all. At this point, mention must be made about the holy nature of these trees. Neither man nor beast ever show a sour face or committed any act of anger in the vicinity. Any act of untoward behavior was regarded as taboo.

Words were superfluous for communication between these lovers. Although the dialects of the two tribes were different, they soon learned to understand each other and communicated completely. Anyhow, love has its own language.

They swore their undying love for each other, neglecting two facts. The first was, a dozen moons hence Chief Acarai promised his only daughter, Shea's hand in marriage, to the great warrior Kanuku.

The second was that though there was no open war between the two peoples for many moons, an old enmity, (the cause of which the people have forgotten or never knew), still existed among them, and marriage, or even the thought of the tribes mixing, was a "no, no!" and regarded as miscegenation on both sides.

Since everything was in abundance, the people on both sides of the river were loath to leave the area. This served the lovers amply. Their love was so strong that they rose from their sleepless beds earlier and earlier every night as if tempting Providence.

One night not long after, Kanuku, having noticed the glow on Shea's countenance, could not get it out of his mind. So while he was still awake with this perplexing thought, he noticed from the corner of his eye a movement. In a moment he was wide-awake. He readily recognized the shape and size of his promised bride. He started to follow to see what he could. Kanuku nearly blew his top when he discovered this clandestine and potentially dangerous encounter. He would have, there and then, slain Kako with his bare hands. Such was his ire, but Kanuku did not become the great warrior that he was by acting precipitately. He held his hand and with fire in his veins and gall in his throat, he closed his eyes and wandered aimlessly for some time before returning to camp when the volcano in his head had subsided somewhat.

Sleep did not claim his tortured soul for the rest of the night. So he did not fail to notice the stealthy and assumed return of Shea. When he caught the radiance of her face, his gall arose anew. Presently he went to the place where the Chief Amerai was, and awakened him. He related to the Chief what he had seen with great embellishment. The Chief was so enraged that one of those lowlander scums, one of those eater of the tacuma beetle, those eater of worms should have the temerity to steal his only daughter away from him!

Forgoing breakfast, the Chief summoned his five sons and narrated the insult to their sister. The Chief embellished the story further and suggested that these eaters of worms bewitched their sister.

The strategy worked out was to lie in wait the next night and catch the culprit in the act and water the soil with his blood.

After nightfall and after the third crowing of the maam, Shea arose, put her stole around her shoulder and left to keep her rapturous rendezvous. Luna illuminated the heavens in brilliant light, silhouetting the trees as a background to a surreal scenery. Her departure did not go un-noticed by the father and the jealous Kanuku. The sons and the duo, armed with stout war-clubs waited for some time and then, bending low, silently stalked their way to a point adjoining the meeting place of the lovers.

Kako, already there, was unwrapping from his garape a choice piece of cooked paca, which he had saved from his dinner. He was unarmed except for his flensing knife, which he now had in his hand with the tender morsel impaled offering it to his love. Shea for her part was coyly turning the morsel to Kako's mouth with the knife in her hand and the meat tenderly nearing Kako's lips. There was a sudden rush of feet towards them.

With upraised clubs they descended on the unarmed lovers. Kanuku aimed a mighty blow at the head of Kako with his mighty purple-heart war-club. Kako anticipated the move and adroitly sidestepped, swinging his body and at the same time getting his hand around the attacker's neck where he held on in a half-nelson. In the forward rush and the sagacious avoidance of the first fatal blow, the two brothers, with raised clubs to brain Kako, missed and, instead, knocked each other out. The other brother mistaking the mix-up started belaboring the two on the ground inextricably locked one with the other. In the confusion the Chief and son did not care that they clubbed Kanuku as much as Kako.

Shea, meanwhile, stood slightly bent with the knife in her right hand and her left knuckles across her mouth, biting her bloodless flesh, with the knife still tightly clutched in her right hand. Both Kako and Kanuku were knocked senseless by this time. They both were prostrate at the feet of Shea when the Chief Amerai, her father, emerged from the shadows and calmly knocked the brains out of Kako with one mighty blow, scattering bones and grey matter in all directions.

No one at that moment could fathom what was passing through Shea's mind like the explosion of nuclear energy! With a shrill high feral scream and one mighty leap, she sprang upon the prostrate and lifeless form of Kako. The three brothers, now dazed and awake, pried her loose. They gazed into her glazed and ghastly eyes, horrified that a knife protruded from her left breast.

When the morning sun rose lancing its keen rays over the escarpment, a strange scene greeted the landscape. All the leaves from all the trees were on the ground. When the light was bright enough for all to see, a great whirlwind arose and raked all the leaves towards the central tree. The leaves completely covered the corpses of the lovers to a depth of many feet. A great grey cloud covered the sun and a hot wind blew across the terrain. Suddenly there was a great flash of lightning and the savannah grass caught afire. Everything, including the leaves, was devoured in the sweeping flames. The trees of life were burnt into grotesque shapes, and low and behold, when the rains returned and the branches sprouted their leaves, they were no more heart-shaped, smooth and shiny. They grew to be very rough and hard with a very sandy surface. They became ovate, curly and ugly. The gnarled branches never regained their former shape but remain like broken and twisted limbs attached like appendages from an equally grotesque trunk.

The wood, which started fire for all and sundry became so silicated, that, even among the best flammable materials, it never blazes or even glows. It has now become useless even as a source of fuel.

What of the saccharine and nectar-like fruits that gave sustenance to man and beast alike? Never again, neither the semblance of bud nor flower, ever greeted the rising sun, or introduced the morning dew bursting in myriads of rays of light to delight the heart. Even the flowers became drab muddy miniature inflorescences, which only the grossest of insects will feign to visit.

This, according to pre-Colombian savannah lore, is the latest in a series of botanical withdrawal from the utilitarianism of animals. The frailty and destructive habits of man's base emotions, resulting in rabid and carnal jealousy and slaughter, have resulted in the destruction of his Eden. Probably if the Provider of the First Garden had been so severe or extensive with 'The Tree of the Fruit of Life,' then today we would have evolved a holier breed of humanity.

Note: This story was told to me by an old acquaintance who I was privileged to call friend. He once graced my humble abode during my sojourn in the Rupununi. "Man's inhumanity to man, spurred by the greed of the flesh, is the cause of man's suffering and downfall," my guest averred.

(Above: Curatella Americana image. Source: www.tropical.theferns.info.com

****

How Unity Finally Came to The Macushi And Wapishana

Pio was destined to be great, someone of substance, some-one who was pre-ordained to do great deeds. The day he was born marked the end of the protracted drought that had devastated the llanos for two years in succession.

Although the day dawned with the usual brilliance, orange and red in the east, forecasting another hot and sultry day, no one suspected that, lurking in both the Roraima Highlands and behind the Kanukus, were two great masses of supersaturated air. As the northern savannah heated up, the slight "nor'easter", having reached the basin, quickly absorbed the heat and started quickly rising with ever increasing velocity to the frigid regions of the cold atmosphere.

(Above: The Kanuku Mountains of Guyana. Source: www.guyanacityguide.com)

The great convection movement served to pull down the mountain air from both sides with its superabundance of moisture and transported it into the upper strata.

Suddenly, in the early afternoon, thunderheads started to form. Lightning started to flash from cloud to somber cloud and from the base cloud to the earth as electrical energy raced to discharge. The breezes became fiercer and the clouds darker as great thunderheads developed and prepared to deluge the landscape with wanton abundance.

This started six hours of unceasing downpour. As the huge drops spattered upon the sere earth and the scraggly cayahbay bent before the strong winds, savannah animals could be seen scurrying toward the dried-up streams to take advantage of the scant shelter that the sparse vegetation might offer. The mirishi, with their brittle stems, snapped like matchsticks at their roots and rolled ahead of the winds, like tumble weeds before the wind, to lodge among the restraining roots of more sturdy plants, to be collected as firewood when the weather got better.

As the sky was being cleared of its clouds, from the highest peak of the Kanukus rolled a great wall of fire. This ball seemed to cavort among the various village huts, then to hover on top of Kamakusa's hut, then rose straight into the air and disintegrated into a million sparks of brilliance, before disappearing altogether.

The phenomenon did not escape the villagers' attention, some of who were outdoors in this respite to survey any damage done to their roofs and outhouses.

Unknown to most laymen, this was seen by all the Chiefs and Peimen in the surrounding villages -- from Arewa and Moco-moco, Kumu and Bomfin, and Parishara and Tabatinga. They all knew this as an omen, and therefore all the Peimen journeyed to Nappi from which they knew that the sign had originated. All the other villages of the north Savannahs had representatives en route there, making Nappi their destination.

They each bore gifts since they each sensed that someone great had entered the land. Hasn't this been foretold generations ago when dissention started among the tribes at the confluence of the Maranon and Negro when the tribes parted? At the very moment that the St. Elmo's dissipated into the heavens, Pio entered into the world, a robust eleven pounds infant, squalling at the top of his lungs.

The father was escorted out of the hammock by some village elders, after having experienced all the pangs of childbirth as the mother did. Great feasting and other celebrations took up the entire week. Visitors continued to pour into the village and deposited their presents under the white cotton hammock in which Pio lay, being gently rocked by doting elders and children alike as they gazed on his cherubic countenance.

North of the mountains and especially at the foothills where Nappi was located copious showers adequately soaked the arid land. Word soon spread to the South about the birth of the baby at such a momentous time as well as the signs and omens that preceded the birth. Now only scant showers barley settled the dust in the South, so the people felt that those of the North had worked some sort of strange magic on them. Always, when rain fell, it fell with equal intensity in both North and South. The Northerners must have very strong medicine to keep the rains for themselves they reasoned.

Little did they know that, with less fanfare, that within the week, there would be so much rain as to inundate their entire area and cause poisonous snakes and other vermin to invade their benabs.

Inadvertently, they attributed this too to the stronger medicine of the North.

These seeds of distrust were sown eons ago in their minds and gained impetus and grew larger as time went by, especially if conditions seemed different between North and South. Any adverse thing that occurred that caused a difference between the two sides of the mountains between the two tribes was attributed to the stronger medicine and magic of the other.

As time went by, Pio grew up quickly to be an extraordinary young man. His beauty, bravery and fame spread far and wide. This bronze giant had a full head of ebon hair that he took extraordinary care of, and of which he was very proud. It emitted a sort of halo when seen in certain light, and was the pride of the owner. Pio grew up to be the strongest and most agile wrestler among all the villages of the North. Whether his opponents were more robust or stronger, he always triumphed over them.

Although there was no open hostility between them, both the Macushi and the Wapishana, as if by tacit agreement, always hunted on their side of the Kanuku, planted on their own side, and even fished in the streams on their side of the mountain range, thus making the water-shed an invisible boundary.

Even when a kamma was shot on one side and limped across the divide to die in the undeclared enemy territory, the enemy did not follow the quarry into their territory. The opposite hunters on the other hand left the animal to die and waste, suspecting a ploy to poison them.

The time eventually came for Pio to choose a wife. In all the annual wrestling matches in the Northern villages, he kept his eyes out for a favorable maiden, but he did not see even one whom he would deign to favor with his attention. Everywhere he went all the nubile maidens went out of their way to attract his attention but he seemed not to spot a favorable one.

Although communication between North and South was minimal, this did not stop word from filtering through of a legendary maiden known as Ayacanora whose charms and femininity were beyond compare. So testified any who has ever even espied her. Young and old pandered to her wishes and held her in such adoration that all the young men felt inadequate to ask her hand in marriage. This caused Ayacanora no alarm or generated any hint of inadequacy. It only served to increase her self-imposed narcissism and gave her the idea that no one in the tribe was worthy of her charms. So as fate would have it, in both tribes were two very marriageable persons not being content with what they had.

As time went by, the elders became worried, especially Kamakusa, Pio's father, who felt that the splendid genes of his lineage would waste itself in oblivion, and that his only son would not bear the family an heir. The father therefore called the elders of the tribe after having ascertained that Pio has not found a suitable bride among his people. Pio agreed that it was time that he should have found a wife but told the elders as he has confessed to his father. He confessed that he was even giving marriage a thought. They stayed long into the night discussing and making suggestions to Pio of all the marriageable maidens available. To each suggestion Pio seemed to find some fault in the character or some physical trait that he felt was not an appropriate one to bequeath to a future offspring.

Late into the wee hours of the morning, with a quizzical and somber and faraway look in his eyes, a great uncle of Pio awoke as from a reverie and smiled broadly as some sort of psychic as realization dawned in his fertile mind. He was about to put the parakari bowl to his lips when realization struck him. He put the bowl down. The stoic look left his visage and was replaced by a rare and broad smile and, with great introspection, raised his hand as to accentuate the silence and spoke. "I think I know where the heart of my nephew is destined," he silently intoned with a voice of finality. The somnolent circle of elders seemed to be galvanized awake at the utterance of this sentence.

"And where is that?" enquired the now wide-awake Kamakusa, with his eyes now focused on his son's limpid countenance. All eyes were now turned questioningly to the sober visage of the uncle who uttered another sentence more like a sentence, rather than a question to Pio.

(Above: A group of Wapishana dancers, including beautiful women and men of valor. Source: www.stabroeknews.com

"It is the legendary Ayacanora, isn't it, my son?

After a long pause, Pio lifted his now blazing face and said, "I guess so my revered uncle".

Everyone was now wide awake as the firelight played hide and seek on the now agitated faces. Only the father seemed to be stoically silent and uttered a phrase that brought a semblance of levity to the seeming agitation.

"But how?" he queried.

In olden times, in so called civilized Old World societies, a situation like this would have been legitimate reason to go to war. Many wars were started for less frivolous reasons. The patriarch of the home rose and asked everyone to sleep on it seeing that it was already very late into the night.

"We will meet at sun down tomorrow to discuss a solution". He said with finality.

At dusk the gathering assembled in the meeting hut. After some intense discussion it was decided that they must send a delegation to the Chief of the Wapishanas for discussion and to declare their mission. Three elders were chosen and appropriate gifts were selected to be given to the Chief, and the Peiman was consulted for the most auspicious date and time for the encounter. It was decided that, the next morning before dawn, was the most auspicious time to set out.

Great was the agitation when the outer guards of the Wapishana sentries spotted the strangers approaching their domain; runners dispatched to the Chief brought the message that the interlopers must be stopped. As if from empty air the emissaries suddenly found themselves surrounded by a dozen sturdy menacing warriors. With palms facing outwards, Kamakusa, as leader of the group, made it known that their mission was one of peace with the Chief and the father of Ayacanora. The warriors suspected treachery, but when they realized that these were three old men, they hastily dispatched another runner to the Chief with the new message.

The Chief hastily summoned Ayacanora's father to his presence and asked, what, if anything, he knew of the three emissaries.

As Ayacanora's father was a respected member of the clan and of the tribe, and a relative of the Chief, he accompanied the Chief to the place where the emissaries were detained. A suitable hut was earmarked for the discussion that was about to take place.

The hut was surrounded with warriors. The men were refreshed as guests, where after they stated their mission. Of course they so praised the valor and fine qualities of Pio that the normally stoic faces of the Chief and his companions evinced traces of interest. At the end the Chief spoke,

"We have heard of the prowess of your son, Pio, through many itinerant nomads who occasionally trade with us. We do not believe that one so young as you speak of, at his age, can be of the reputation that you have just advertised. We do not believe all that you have said. We also have many great warriors who perform many great feats of strength and daring, but none has Ayacanora seen fit to be her life partner. However we invite you to be our guests tonight. We will have to consult with our medicine men. However one question bothers us. How did your son, Pio, know of our princess?"

Kamakusa answered that the reputation and beauty of Ayacanora were brought over by none other than Pio himself. This seemed quite intriguing. It caught the hosts by surprise so that it was decided that the next day be set for further discussion.

The visitors retired to the benab specially prepared for special guests with two stalwarts to cater for their every comfort. The hosts, meanwhile, did not sleep early, but conferred long into the night. They enlisted in the family conference the chief Peiman. Discussion, however, seemed not to resolve the issue at hand. Then Peiman asked for a respite and went into a trance to consult with the good spirits. All remained absolutely quiet while the Peiman was in his trance and all held their breaths awaiting the outcome, especially the father of Ayacanora, knowing how fickle and fastidious was his daughter.

When the Peiman awoke from his trance, he seemed to be in a daze and the father had to force him to talk.

"I see", he said, "the brilliant golden orb of the morning sun. From north and south two hearts were gushing crimson blood, which seemed to mingle in the center but parting at the bottom. Then out of the morning mists at the bottom there arose the greatest, whitest harpy heart with wings outstretched and with the feathers at the tips of the huge wing curved inwards. The harpy heart was a wounded dove. As the dove's blood fell it did not touch the ground but became the mists that arose as bright clouds on both sides of the mountains. While loath to mix, the red and white mists united just like when the harpy draws its wings together towards its breast."

After he had finished speaking, the Peiman collapsed on the ground and fell into a deep sleep. Both the Chief and the rest followed the Peiman's example and retired to their hammocks.

After morning ablutions and a hearty breakfast, the guests were taken on a tour of the secret hill of mica and other sites that only reached the outside world in legends. Meanwhile the Chief called his advisors to decide what answer he must give the strangers.

Councilmen, whose sons evinced interest in Ayacanora, quickly put their preferences aside when the Peiman related his dream. All agreed to see this great Pio whose valor at wrestling and prowess at other activities was legendary.

The visitors were laden with gifts and invited to bring Pio and an entourage of young men for a visit.

Was Ayacanora consulted? When the news was taken to her through her mother, she first felt elated, then succumbed to a fit of rage. However, when this rage died down, curiosity bettered her reluctance, and she acquiesced to bow to her father's wishes since he thought so highly of the stranger who he has never seen before. Her wise father, she thought, must have very good reason to want to see Pio. However, in Ayacanora's fertile mind, neither filial obligation nor obedience, but coquetry caused her to acquiesce to the suggestion of her father. In her mind she knew, as all of the female sex knew, that once Pio would have picked up the glove, and Eros planted the arrow in his heart he will do all of her bidding, regardless of the consequences to himself.

The day came when Pio, his father and relatives and friends arrived at Mountain Foot, as was previously arranged between the parties. They were met by a contingent of elders all bedecked in ceremonial regalia. The visitors were escorted for a long time into the heartland of the Wapishana country. There, in a newly constructed hut with newly spun hammocks, the guests were made comfortable.

Pio was so nervous that he did not sleep a wink for the entire night. Early next morning as the entourage was finishing their morning's ablutions, an emissary arrived to say that the guests were invited to have breakfast at the Chief's benab.

Pio's father led the procession behind the guides in single file as the Rupununi sun rose on the eastern brow of the Kanuku Mountains in all their splendor. Decked out in their best clothes as was befitting the occasion, the procession wended its way to the biggest benab. Pio stood out head and shoulders among the regal contingent as a bronze god among lesser earthlings. Other members tried their best to shelter him from the sight of the bystanders but were hardly successful. He towered above all the rest.

The visitors were ushered towards a table of roughly hewn cedar on which was piled the bounty of the land. Although it was only breakfast time, the table was piled with baked lukanani, ollas of

(Above: "The 'sweetest' sweet-water fish, lukanani." Source: www.thingsguyana.com)

thick cream and calabashes of quariad. There were platters of pasowk and deep bowls of tuma. The all-pervading aroma of the benab transported the guests and hosts alike to the realm of dreams.

The guests remained standing while the Chief ambled to the head of the board and invited all to be seated. The South turned their faces towards the North and the North turned their faces towards the South. "Welcome to our humble abode, and may the history we are creating today remain forever in the hearts of our people".

Kamakusa took advantage after the pause to stand up and bow towards his hosts. "Your generosity is very welcome my revered sir. May our first meal together be not only memorable but also be the precursor of our intentions, veracity, honesty, humility and serve to cement the purpose for which we are here." He ended with, "May today be the day foreseen as a new beginning".

"Your eloquence speaks of the honesty within your heart," replied the host. "Let us satisfy our hunger, then we shall get down to your mission among us".

Everyone ate in silence as empty bowls were removed and replenished with filled ones. Finally when all was sated and the dishes were cleared, the entire gathering repaired to the conference hut. There the father of Ayacanora, ensconced in his hand crafted seat at the head of the elongated circle of hosts on one side and guests on the other, raised his hand and asked that, although he already knew of the mission of the visitors, that they state formally why they had come. Whereupon, Kamakusa very calmly got up and with equanimity stated, "The beauty and fame of your esteemed daughter has so captivated my son that he has refused to look favorably on any other maiden. He has vowed to his family that he will marry none but your daughter, hence our mission."

"We have also heard of the prowess of your son," replied Ayacanora's father. "Being face to face with him has justified that reputation. However, only my daughter can give you the answer you seek. She shall be here presently." With that there was a slight whisper as if a cooling zephyr was passing through the benab as a bevy of beauties appeared behind their princess behind the father, as if by magic.

The dim interior of the benab seemed to be brightened and charged with electricity as the young women stood behind their princess who was given a seat next to her father. Pio at first felt a slight nervous reticence as he lifted his eyes to lock with those of Ayacanora. Visible sparks seemed to fly, as the two hearts seemed to pair off on each other. As Ayacanora gracefully lowered her golden fan, (made from the feathers of the cock-of-the-rock), slowly past her ivory throat, Pio was so enthralled that a lump rose in his breast. Time stood still as the fan rested on the cleavage of Ayacanora's breast as primordial emotions transfixed and held the gazes of this dreamily enthralling pair.

(Above: The cock-of-the-rock bird of Guyana (Rupicola rupicola) Source: www.hbw.com/ibc

The silence was so thick, yet poignant with expectancy, that Pio recalled that, if he was called upon to say something he might "have put his foot in his mouth". However, the father turned to the daughter and asked. "My jewel, what do you think of the young man?"

After a short pause it appeared as if Ayacanora seemed to be in deep thought, then the maiden said in an audible whisper, "My father, you have brought me up to respect the mores of our people. If the young man who I do not even know until today will agree and adhere to our traditions, then I think I may look favorably on him".

Having said thus Ayacanora and the maidens withdrew.

Long and hard was the discussion on both sides. At length it was decided that, apart from the normal field cutting, which Pio had to undertake to show that he can take care of a wife, at the coming Cashew Festival, Pio will have to wrestle seven young men to show that he could always defend the one he loves.

Pio readily agreed to all the demands put up by Ayacanora's father, even when some seemed to be beyond reason.

The field cutting was easy compared with bringing back the skull and skin of a jaguar to show that he was a skilled hunter.

As he rested in the guest house alone (the contingent had left to take care of their own chores), rubbing cockerite fat on his aching muscles, the Peiman brought the message to Pio that he must, this night, cleanse himself prior to his fight with the three pairs of warriors and the giant Jurandi who was Ayacanora's chief, but rejected, local suitor.

When the morrow arrived, all was gathered in the square as Pio and his second (a haunch-back who was once hugged by a barim, giant ant-eater, made their way to the arena, Pio's skin glistening with snake oil.)

The first pair was a walkover for Pio. He adroitly sidestepped them and allowed them to knock themselves out in their opposite and headlong rush to grab him. The other pair was wary and tackled Pio in a slightly different manner. He tripped the first one, grabbed the other and threw him in the face of the other as he swung around. It was then that he espied Ayacanora for the first time at the back of the crowd seated on a low stool.

The third pair appeared more formidable, as he now detected a faint smile and a feral light in the eyes of his beloved. Pio now felt the adrenalin surge in his veins and a feeling of invincibility permeated his entire being, mind and soul. Pio summoned all his guile and tact that he had practiced among his people and quickly locked his legs around one of the contestants in a scissor lock, while he locked his muscular arms around the neck of the other in a full nelson. He did not let go until he made sure that he had vanquished both.

Last came the huge Jurandi with his chest like a barrel, his legs like the trunks of locust trees, and arms like two muscular legs. Jurandi had a smile on his face as he tackled Pio and held him in a head-lock trying to turn him to get his shoulder in the dust. Try as he might, Pio could not pull Jurandi's legs from under him, although he had a secure grip. He brought all the pressure he could muster, then suddenly relaxed. This caught Jurandi by surprise. He loosed his grip slightly as Pio slid under him, took his entire weight on his shoulder and heaved him up in the air and threw him with a mighty thud. Jurandi fell on his back and lay still.

Ayacanora's father took Pio by the hand and led him to his daughter, placed his trembling hand in hers and withdrew. Pio felt faint and would have fallen if Ayacanora did not put her hand around his shoulder to steady him.

Accepted into the family, he dispatched runners to the North. After a feasting of seven days, Pio and Ayacanora were united by the two Peimen in holy matrimony. They had many children who did great deeds among their people. But the greatest thing that ever happened was everlasting peace between the Macushi and the Wapishana, which can still be evidenced today.

So it was foretold eons ago by their ancestors!

****

In Quest Of Kashima

The Sipu River starts its descent high up the 2000ft. - 3000ft. valley between the Kamoa Mountains and the Sierra Acarai in southwest Guyana as a gentle trickle. It increases in strength as myriads of streamlets join it as it descends the main valley. It flows north-east for some distance until it is joined on its left bank by the Chodikar and the Talimwau, which greatly increases its volume and makes it navigable to canoes and other small riverain crafts. Another appreciable branch streams on its left bank as the river descends and is called the Wapuau. Opposite this river on the right bank of the Sipu is the settlement of Konashen.

Konashen was not always there. It is now one of the remotest villages in Guyana's hinterland and is peopled by the Wai-wai. These people have been known by different names during different periods of their history, according to which outsider paid a visit to the settlement. They have been diversely referred to by various names like Wai-wai, We-we, White-indians or Indio-de, and Tapioc. According to Nicholas Guppy in his book, *Wai-wai,* page 41, "...pale in complexion these Indians were. Their name Wai-wai is the Wapishana for tapioca, and the Brazilians call them 'Indios de Tapioc' and regard them as 'White Indians'. But the names for themselves is We-we or wood, and means people who live in the forest".

All who has met this tribe will attest to their excellent manners. And one who has lived among the various tribes will readily notice the difference in pigmentation and beauty of the women, especially. Guppy had this to say, "The women were thickset by classical standards, and their breasts were a little full, but even among the middle-aged and elderly ones, there was much beauty".

No one knows with absolute certainty when the tribe arrived at its present location, but legend has it that about two hundred years ago, they travelled from the Aramata region of the New River area near the border with Suriname and settled at their present location some time later.

As they slowly wended their way westward, they encountered and mixed with a new tribe, the Tarumas. These people trace their ancestral origin to the daughter of an anaconda. According to their legends " ...no anaconda was ever harmed by a Taruma, but was regarded as a member of the tribe, addressed as 'uncle', and avoided".

It was sometime after the Wai-wai joined the Tarumas, and the tribes intermingled, that the great rains came. They, the Tarumas, lived at the confluence where the Kassikaityu River joined the Dessekebe (Essequibo), a name derived from the Arawak "Dissichipu".

From the onset of the meeting of the tribes, a section of the older people was dissatisfied with the close intermingling of the tribes, especially that of the young people. They warned of the dire circumstances that will follow. So when the great flood came and all the cultivated fields were inundated, this section exploited the opportunity to attribute this disaster to the "sin" of the free mixing of people.

Then when the younger of the tribes dived under the ever, rising water in the fields to salvage the cassava and yams and other perishables, to at least sustain life, a part of the tribe loaded what they could into their corials, and under a young leader Moiwa, journeyed upriver to their present location at Konashen. The rest of the tribe, most of whom were Tarumas consisting of some very old and some very young, bided their time, and, rather than leaving all that they owned, continued to bear all the hardships that the great flood brought. However, during their greatest time of hardship, the elders returned to the confluence with the Kassikaityu and were never heard of again. It is said that the name of the river originally

94

meant paca, a large succulent rodent in the Taruma language, but sometime later, when the survivors of the flood went in search of their elders, they found not one trace of them. Thereafter, Kassikaityu came to assume the Arawak meaning of, according to Schomburgh and Farabee, *"The River of the Dead"*. "Kassi", is interpreted to mean "the dead", and "kityu" to mean "river". Whatever the meaning, the river still bears the same name today.

Now, according to the legend of the day, the people had been split up into three sections because of the great flood. The Kassikaityu group who perished, The Konashen group under the leadership of Moiwa, and the group that was left between the two, comprising of mostly Tarumas. The water receded after a few weeks and, despite the destruction of the crops, life soon returned to normal.

What both sets of people did not know, however, was, because of the special aspect of the land, during heavy rains, usually after one hundred moons, the upper reaches of the river, especially the Sipu and its branches, will experience great floods But the flood quickly recedes from the upper reaches and remains longer lower down the river as the configuration of the river changes to a gentler slope.

Moiwa carved out his settlement and his village prospered. His erstwhile relatives, whom they had left behind, were now under an able touchau called Fonyuwe. Their village also reverted to its former glory. Communication between the two villages, which was merely cordial at first, assumed greater and greater intimacy as both villages became more and more self-sufficient

Things, however, started to change at Konashen with the arrival of a very old man. Although he wore his hair long, he did not enclose it in the customary tube as the Wai-wai do. His hair, unlike the sleek ebon coif on the other men, was slightly gray and bushy, and hung unkempt down to his shoulders. He was of a nondescript countenance until you observed his deer-set and sunken eyes that seemed to penetrate the inner recesses of the soul of the person on whom his gaze was directed.

Kafka, as he was preferred to be called, had a strange tale to tell. When he arrived, he became the guest of Moiwa's benab and readily fitted himself into the family routine, befriending especially those who seemed to be quite attracted to his unconventional ways.

Kafka had a strange story to tell. When he was questioned from whence he came, he uttered one word, "Kashima". When he was asked where this place was located, he pointed in one general direction towards the mountains. However it was difficult to pinpoint a specific location, since he pointed between earth and sky. So no one could decipher that he meant on top of the mountains, beyond the mountains or in the skies above the mountains.

Every evening the entire tribe, and even the Taruma visitors, would eagerly gather in the communal benab to hear Kafka relate stories of Kashima. Word soon reached the village of Fonyuwe, so it was not unusual for a string of visitors to be ever present to hear Kafka relate his tales. According to him Kashima was the biggest village in all creation. No one had to work since all the trees of the forest were fruit trees that bore in abundance throughout the year. All the fruits were such that, when the branches in the east had blossoms, those in the north had ripe fruits. Simultaneously, those branches of the west had mature fruits, while the branches in the south had young ones. In this manner, fruits were always in abundance.

The cassava had their tubers hanging from their branches and never required any effort to be dug; and so were the sweet potato and other crops. Every house had bees that made honey in one gooby, (dried hollowed out gourd), while they reared their young ones in other goobies hung in other parts of the various benabs.

Hunters had never to go out to search for game. The peccaries and other wild animals regularly go to pick cassava and other food, while the kamma changed his habits and fed by day so that the hunters can readily catch them when they came to gnaw at the sugarcane that grew wild everywhere. Capybara came to graze in the rice grass that grew in the tiny streams that meandered among the huts. Marudi and maam, and powis and duraquarra, used the hanging baskets to lay their eggs. And, since no one ate eggs there was abundance, and there were all kinds of feathered stock that were readily available to eat.

"Above all", intoned Kafka, in his quiet monotone that seemed to penetrate into the remotest corners of the benab, "there are exactly twelve hours of daylight and twelve of night, and the rains fall only in the night. But best of all there are twelve hours of moonlight every night all night from sunset to sunrise."

Now, all these mysterious, inexplicable and impossible happenings so intrigued the listeners that one night, Moiwe asked, "So my revered friend, what kind of people live in Kashima? What are their customs? Are there children? What do people do for recreation?"

This set of questions was fired as a single broadside, and, as might be expected, the spate of words brought silence from everyone. After a respectable pause Kafka replied in barely a whisper, yet for all to hear, "Kashima is what the Great Manitou meant the world to be. There is neither suffering nor any death in Kashima. Yes there are people of all ages and description and their recreation is life".

Fonyuwe, who had sat through many nights in absorbing all that transpired, sipping his "kari" silently, as the bowl was passed from hand to hand, at last ventured his piece. Not to be outdone in gravity and respect, he asked, "and how dear father can we get to Kashima? How must one travel, and what is required for the journey? Fonyuwe passed the bowl to Moiwa as he awaited the old man's reply. Kafka seems to be asleep, but suddenly he seemed to be widely awake as he replied enunciating each word with deliberation: "One gets to Kashima only by giving up the cares of this world and dedicating oneself to the service of others." After a long pause he continued. "Kashima only accepts the children of selflessness. Since no one ever grows old in Kashima, the fear of death is absent. The journey is long and needs the dedication of purpose. The people of Kashima reach their goal after travelling in the path of righteousness and love. There is no special path that takes you there, but once you press forward with goodness in your heart you will eventually enter the great village".

Having said this, a great silence fell upon the gathering as they slowly ponder the Great One's word. As Kafka stopped speaking, a somnolent atmosphere seemed to envelop and permeate the listeners' souls in the great benab. Silently everyone slipped away to his or her hammock to ponder or perhaps dream of Kashima.
The next morning when Moiwe arose, he went across the earthen floor to awaken his guest for the morning's ablution in the river. Kafka's hammock was empty, It is strange he thought that Kafka will go down to the river without him, since this has become a morning ritual. He nevertheless went down to the stream alone. When he returned he went to the guest hut, but no one had seen the storyteller.

Young men went out during the days that ensued, and scoured every trail for clues. None was discovered anywhere. Nothing was taken, not even Kafka's food-bowl, which still rested in the customary place on the shelf. He seemed to have vanished into thin air. He went as he came and was never heard of again.

The appetites of all the members of the tribe were whetted by the words of the visitor. Both Fonyuwe and Moiwe resolved in their minds that they must find Kashima. So it did not seem strange or far-fetched when Moiwe broached the subject with his Taruma kin.

Exactly two moons later, a dozen able-bodied men were gathered, and after many pep talks by both chiefs, they were told that they must immediately commence the search for the fabulous village. The men must however plan their journey in such a way that they must return within a dozen moons and not later.

Early the next morning the expedition set out in the general direction of Mount Faiafun where the gnarled fingers of Kafka seemed to have been pointing when he was questioned about the location of Kashima.

They left Konashen, headed south, and crossed Mount Faiafun in the Acarai watershed. Many were the adventures as they went over the watershed and went into the Taurini. The men spent some time at Manata's village making discreet enquiries. On this branch of the Mapuera River they learnt that, if they continued they will meet the "Mother of Waters," which they did not wish to do. At the village on the Mapuera, however, their belief was reinforced as similar tales of the fabulous Kashima seemed to have been spread not only there, but throughout the entire area. Some of the men from Manata's village joined the expedition, but soon left when hardship struck. They left the river and crossed Mount Faiafun and came eventually to the river Tutumo, and crossed Imai Bau. They trudged across the Mara Yaku to Tiko Tirir. They journeyed further east to Shiruru Tirir where they waited for a few days to recoup and stock up on provisions. They intended to cross the 1200ft. Sierra Irikoume to join another branch of the mighty Amazon which some call the Rio Alto Trombetas, but others call it Carfuini.. They found some difficulty in ascending one of the branches of the Trombetas back to the watershed of the Acarai. After losing one of their canoes and some provisions, they almost starved as the area was devoid of any game. There were no paths even to give the indication that people had once passed there. This area, they reasoned, is a far cry from where Kashima could be situated, and hence must be elsewhere. Kashima they visualized must be away from any lowland; therefore they decided to look in the higher areas as befits the location of a village of the stature of which they visualized Kashima to be.

They now climbed back to the watershed and made their journey eastward along the backbone of the mountains. Although they did not know it, they had journeyed as far as the land that their ancestors left long ago in the region of the Aramata River. They were now well off because of the abundance of game, but they found no inhabited Big Village. However they found signs that the land was once inhabited.

Nine moons had now passed since they left their home on the Sipu it was high time that they turn their faces homeward. They followed the ridges along the watershed westwards for two moons until they reached familiar territory on the Chodikar. They eventually reached Konashen where they reported to Moiwa and hastily summoned Fonyuwe.

Their journey was embellished with many hardships, imagined and real, and many adventures. Long and interesting was the saga of their journey, but still missing was the reality of the fabulous and legendary Kashima, the Eden and Valahalla, the abode of those who dedicated their lives to the service of their fellow man.

If today anyone was to visit the remotest villages of the extreme south of the People of the Wood, they may still hear, around the camp-fire, during story-time when the stomach is sated, and especially if the kari bowl is moving hand to hand, the wonderful and unsuccessful "Quest for Kashima".

(The writer's Observation: How different from the story of Kashima is our promise of Heaven?).

(Above: the ite palm tree of the Rupununi Savannahs, Guyana; also known as the Aquache Palm – Mauritia Flexuosa. Source: www.alamy.com

****

Why Melinda's Cheeks are Red?

Mamma Edwin, Papa Edwin and little Melinda Edwin were returning from their farm at Kumu where they spent their week-ends making farine. Rain did not fall for a very long time and the land was sere. Dust devils played on the flat savannah terrain as the eyes were dazzled by the shimmering heat.

Papa Edwin was ahead of the trio with his bow in his hand and his machete at his side. Seven year-old Melinda was a little behind her papa, sometimes chasing the yellow butterflies that alighted on the dusty path seeking the scant minerals to maintain their metabolism. Mama Edwin brought up the rear with her warishi filled to capacity with a half-bunch of cokerite and other goodies from the farm along with an exotic bead apron, which Mama Edwin always seemed to be working on.

(Above: Amerindian woman with warishi on her back. Source: www.guyanatimesgy.com)

That weekend though Papa Edwin went far into the hills in quest of game, he was not successful in even shooting a duraquarra for the pot.

As they travelled on the trail in the afternoon heat with the gentle wind in their faces, out of the haze not far in front of them, from behind a bush, there appeared a blur of color.

Meat for the pot he visualized! Both Melinda and her father saw this at the same instant. Both started to move faster; Melinda's face broadened into a wide smile as she hastened towards the blur shouting "Toco"! "Toco"!

Papa Edwin unstrung an arrow from his back, put it to his bow and let fly. Great was his surprise to see the arrow miss by a very wide margin, and flew in a direction it was not even intended to. This made him look at his bow to see if something was wrong with it.

By this time Melinda had caught up with Papa Edwin and was about to shout "stop", when Papa let fly with another arrow. This second arrow missed by a much wider margin.

Papa Edwin was so surprised that he did not notice that Melinda had darted forward and was about to over-take the Toco.

Papa Edwin who could shoot a darting golden throated humming bird to adorn his quiver, had hardly ever missed a target, and was very grateful that strangers were not around to witness his calamity.

Melinda seemed to have disappeared from his sight behind a hazy wall. When next he saw her, she was cradling in her arms the biggest Toco ever seen in the savannahs.

The Toco seemed half-dead from the long drought. Its huge beak was wide open and he was panting for breath. Its eyes were closed as if in prayers, and the great wings hung lifelessly at its sides. The only sign of life was a slight jerking of its tail, as if it was giving voice to its mate in death.

Papa's first reaction when he reached Melinda's side was to grab Toco and wring its flaccid neck. Maybe the shock that he had twice missed, stayed his hand.

Toco seemed to be residing comfortably in Melinda's arm as they resumed their journey homewards. By this time Mama Edwin had reached the two of them.

She looked at the great bird in Melinda's arm and seemed to notice something the others did not see. The great bird had opened one eye and winked secretly at Mama as if to say, "Aye, now I have met the whole family". Nothing else of interest happened on the way home. At last they reached their benab as the heat of the day was just abating. Melinda found an old basket and lined it with soft materials she found around the benab and put Toco to rest. She opened Toco's great bill and poured some cool water down the parched throat. Toco opened its eyes once and went back to sleep. As Mama Edwin prepared the evening meal, Melinda took some cokerite, carefully peeled the hard outer skin and scraped the tender milky flesh into a small calabash. She took the milky sap, opened Toco's bills, and forced it down Toco's throat. The bird tried and painfully swallowed as Melinda gently rubbed its throat and back. When she was finished she gave the bird a little more water, and returned it to its bed in the basket. Twice during the night Toco let out sharp sounds as if he was in the forest. After that all was peaceful. When Melinda fell into her deepest sleep, she seemed to be wide awake, with Toco sitting on the rope of her hammock. Toco seemed to be speaking to Melinda. "Melinda", he said, " you are the kindest and most compassionate person I have ever seen walking in the savannah. Without thinking you took me in. You fed me even before you had eaten. Although this is a dream Melinda, you will remember it in the morning."

Melinda snuggled tighter between the folds of her blanket as if to say, "Oh Toco, you flatter me".

When the family awoke the next morning, Melinda peeked in the basket to see Toco. Toco opened both eyes, looked sideways at Melinda and then hopped weakly on the rim of the basket.

When mama and Melinda returned from the creek, Melinda fed Toco and sat down to her own breakfast of bake and tapioca pudding.

As Toco became stronger he started to follow Melinda everywhere she went. When Melinda went to the well with her saucepan to get some drinking water, Toco will hop and make short flights to and from the well. In the mornings Toco went with Mama and Melinda to the creek and sat on the bank while the duo splashed in the water. Melinda often took water in her mouth and sprayed Toco with fine mists.

About six months later when Mama Edwin was returning from a neighbor's house where she went to visit a sick child, she was greatly surprised to see about a dozen other toucans perched in a circle on the cashew tree in the yard with Toco in the center. She was surprised because she knew that toucans are normally solitary birds. At most she surmised they may travel in twos or threes; but right in front of her eyes there was their Toco, surrounded by more than a dozen others. They appeared to be in deep conversation. So Mama gently retreated to the neighbors to tell them what she had just witnessed.

She promptly returned with her neighbor to find the cashew tree empty, and Toco quietly resting on the usual perch by the low door with his beak tucked snugly under one wing pretending to be asleep.

When the two women entered the benab both Melinda and Papa Edwin were inside. Melinda was peeling cockerite and Papa was half asleep in his hammock. When Mama told them what she had seen, both father and daughter swore that Toco was all the time dozing on his perch, and, both of them could have readily noticed it if it had moved. One day Melinda missed Toco as she went to fetch water from the well. When she returned, she searched the basket, the cashew tree, looked at the top of the benab and everywhere she felt Toco might be. Nowhere did she spy Toco. "This is strange", she thought since Toco never missed feeding time.

Toco was missing for the whole day. Everyone felt sad, especially Melinda who sat in the doorway with her chin on her chest staring languidly into space. However, towards evening when the family was sitting under the cashew tree, in the approaching darkness, wordless with their own thoughts, Melinda started to sob silently. Papa Edwin stopped working on the piece of wood that he was carving into a toy. Without thinking, he was shaping the piece of wood into the beak of a toucan. Mama Edwin had a frame between her legs stringing beads. They both suspended their activities as the sob from Melinda penetrated the gloom. Melinda had a faraway look in her eyes as a huge teardrop silently cut a streak from her eye down her right cheek. Suddenly, as if in answer to her silent cry, as she looked up she shouted, "Look, papa", pointing at a point at a peak in the Kanukus. Two other pairs of eyes joined hers and focused on the point where her hand was pointing. There, in the middle of a circle of birds, shone the dark blue and red wings of one that was clearly larger than all the rest.

As they looked, the middle bird rose straight up and peeled off from the flock, and made a beeline towards the trio. The rest of the birds, as if in respect to a great one, gently floated down towards the forest canopy and was soon swallowed up in its dark green embrace.

Toco flew straight to its perch, climbed down and went to Melinda who presently fed him some soaked farine, after cooing. After Toco was finished eating, he climbed on his perch as if nothing has happened, looking as innocent as could be.

That night, when all was asleep, Toco climbed down from the perch and climbed up the rope of Melinda's hammock. She was awake in an instant. Very quietly Toco started to speak to Melinda in human language. "Melinda", he began very quietly, as if not to alarm her that he could speak. "I must say farewell to you and your family who were very kind to me. When Mama said she saw a number of toucans in the cashew tree, she was right. The time was not then ripe for me to tell you what I am telling you now. You see, Melinda, today it was decided by all my people that I must return to lead them. Since I came to live with you they were leaderless, and they found it very hard to survive without my leadership. You must know now Melinda, that I am King of all the Tocos". Melinda made as if to speak, but Toco crept down the hammock rope and laid its tip of its beak on Melinda's lips. Toco continued, "Men are destroying our homeland with their activities at an unprecedented rate, and therefore I must lead my people further and further a-field to find sustenance if we are to survive. However, this is beside the point. Your people and mine have co-existed side by side for centuries. They are not to blame. It is the newcomers. You surely have to join their ranks one of these days. They have been exploring and have found oil where we live. If they are not careful enough they will destroy the environment with all the activities that soon will follow. Not only your people and mine will be destroyed, but their greed will surely destroy all of us, starting with us the most vulnerable and unrepresented ones.

Melinda sat up in her hammock. In the adjoining hammocks Mama and Papa were snoring away.

Toco, now silent, hopped on Melinda's shoulder as she went to the bucket to slake her now dry throat and lips. Melinda was not thirsty because her throat was dry, but because of the intense emotions that Toco has caused to pass through her mind. As she returned to her hammock, Toco once again hopped on its side and continued. "Melinda, as we go to the creek in the morning, bathe me with the spray from your mouth for the last time. When you have finished I will touch both of your cheeks with my bill. I will fly straight up into the air after that. I will also open my wings and fall to earth as you saw me when first we met. After that tell Mama to look keenly. My people will rise from the forests to welcome me. As you return to your benab, tell Mama what I have told you; and when you go in go straight to your mirror and look. What you see will serve two purposes. Firstly, it will serve as a reminder to work towards the idea of preserving your homeland and mine; and secondly, it will remind you that you once helped a King. You will be proud of this always. One last thing Melinda, all your girl children will inherit the gift that I have bestowed on you".

As was said in the darkness, all happened in the light of the morning sun. Melinda, at first, seemed to have forgotten, but when the first rays of the sun stole over the mountains and lit up the savannah in its iridescent splendor, Mama, Melinda and Toco wended their way to the shimmering creek.

When they were finished bathing, Toco hopped on his favorite rock. It was then that Melinda remembered. She filled her mouth with water and sprayed Toco. The water tasted salty. Melinda did not realize that her tears were mixed with the water. When she was finished, Toco gently touched both of Melinda's cheeks with his rosette bill, rose straight into the air, did as promised, and winged his way towards the welcoming committee waiting silently over the dark foliage of the somber mountains.

Mama picked up her bucket of washing water and journeyed homewards. She stopped and looked in the direction of Melinda's gaze. As she looked, from afar the dark wings of Toco flashed rays of golden sparks as he winged his way towards the mountains. Suddenly there rose from the still dark mountainside a host of toucans into the now glancing rays of the morning sun.

Toco flew straight to the host. Into the center of the circle he flew as they hovered a moment in welcome. Then up into the bright sunshine they flew and disappeared over the now brilliant treetops.

Mama Edwin seemed awed, but nearly fainted when she looked at Melinda. Both of Melinda's cheeks were now the color of the bill of Toco. Mama said nothing as they slowly wended their way homewards from the creek in the now brilliantly lit savannah.

As they entered the benab Papa Edwin rolled in his hammock and planted both his feet firmly on the earthen floor. He paid little attention in the dim interior until they sat down to breakfast. As he looked at Melinda he realized that someone was missing. "Where is Toco"? He asked no one in particular. Melinda's hand went to her cheek as if in answer to her father's question. They ate in silence. Mama Edwin busied herself to take Melinda to her first day of school.

If today, you visit the Village of St. Ignatius next to Arewa and happen to see two little girls with rosette cheeks, romping and playing as any tomboy in a most jovial way, know that they are Melinda's twins and the promise of King Toco.

****

Aunt Edwina's Powis

The day uncle George gave Aunt Edwina a powis chick for her birthday, she was so overjoyed that tears of gladness ran down her rosy cheeks.

Since her two grown sons were in the city going to High School, there seemed to be an emptiness in her heart and a sort of loneliness, especially when uncle George went to the farm to do any planting, or even reap produce for sale, or household use.

Aunt Edwina cradled the half-naked chick in one hand, feeling the heart beating against the soft ribs. She took down an old basket in which she used to put eggs, found one of uncle George's old shirt and made a cozy nest for the chick. She placed the basket on a table next to which a matapi and a quake hung. There she could always keep an eye on the chick as she attended to her household chores.

Before uncle George returned from the Trade Store in Lethem, faint pee pee-ping sounds could be heard emanating from the homely basket. Aunt Edwina realized that the chick was hungry.

Aunt Edwina took a bowl, put some milk in it, and then crushed some cassava bread into the milk, making a delicious and appetizing gruel. She took the chick from the basket, and set the bowl in front of it on the kitchen table. The chick only trembled but did not touch the food. She tried to force some down between the chick's beak but it kept turning its head aside, and did not eat.

Aunt Edwina suddenly remembered how the villagers raised their young parrot chicks that they would occasionally bring home. She put some cassava and milk in her mouth and chewed it. She held the chick in both hands, brought it up to her face and fed the chick with her tongue. The chick hungrily snatched the chewed cassava and swallowed it. Aunt Edwina continued to feed the chick thus until it refused any more. She then returned the chick to the basket and continued with her chores.

When uncle George returned, he brought with him six yards of chicken mesh. Aunt Edwina told uncle George how difficult it was to feed the chick and how she accomplished her task. Uncle George smiled knowingly and thought that the chick was already being spoiled.

At aunt Edwina's birthday everyone took a peek at the basket and remarked what a remarkable chick it was. Someone suggested naming the chick. A contest was quickly set up, and everyone was given a scrap of paper. The prize was that the person, whose name was accepted for the chick, would be given the chance to feed it.

Everyone was told to choose a name that could be applied to either a male or a female since no one could tell the sex of the chick at such an early stage. The entries were collected and after a close-headed discussion among the three judges, they finally settled on the name "Velvet". This name might have seemed appropriate to the judges because they might have visualized that when the chick grew up the feathers would resemble dark velvet.

The winner was Kako who promptly took Velvet out of the basket and proceeded to feed it until its hunger was sated.

Velvet had a very healthy appetite and before the end of the month it was over one pound in weight. Velvet adopted Rover, the family dog, as a surrogate parent and Rover was more than willing to oblige. Velvet followed Rover around whenever this was possible, or waited patiently for him to return when he went out with uncle George.

Velvet soon learnt to eat household scraps, and even ate with Rover from his dish when he was fed. This was very strange since Rover never permitted a single chicken to even steal a scrap from his bowl. Rover seemed to have developed a strong bond for

Velvet since he allowed the bird to eat from his dish.

Velvet grew to be a real beauty. His feathers were a shiny midnight black with a patch of white feathers under its tail. Everyone now recognized it as a male by its shape and the recurved ruff on its head. Two golden wattles on both sides of its white and yellow beak turned pink when Velvet was agitated, and the ruff on his head moved in waves, and sometimes stood on end.

Velvet lived a life of ease as he strutted, sometimes flying away and spending whole days among the trees of the galleria forest of the Moco-moco Creek.

One night uncle George was awakened when he heard Velvet crowing in powis language. Uncle George did not pay much notice to this since he was very busy during the days escorting his sons to various locations in the day and came home very tired in the nights. His sons were home for the long August vacation and uncle George was escorting them to friends. Eventually when they left and uncle George returned from the airport, he quickly noticed the crest-fallen visage of Velvet as if he missed the boys.

As aunt Edwina and uncle George were having lunch, they discussed Velvet's welfare. They soon came to the conclusion that Velvet was lonely and needed company. Velvet even gave up riding on Rover's back when Rover was around. The family decided to take Velvet to their farm in the foothills of the Kanuku to see if he could find such company in the nearby forests.

On the very first day Velvet returned with a mate, and slept the night on the roof of the camp with his friend, instead of his open cage in the camp.

The next morning when uncle George called Velvet, tempting him with some cracked corn, his mate did not come down from the roof, but remained there "pee pee-ing" with outstretched neck in a most curious manner. Uncle George however threw down more corn that was sufficient for Velvet, then made his way to his nearby field. When he looked back he saw Velvet and his companion winging their way to the high forest.

Uncle George stayed at his farm for the whole week. During all this time the two birds went in the forest in the day and returned to roost on the roof of the camp during the night.

When it was time to return home, uncle George opened Velvet's cage, put some corn in it and waited. Velvet seemed to sense the situation, so he daintily walked into the cage. Uncle George closed the cage and loaded it along with his provisions into the jeep.

Velvet's friend stayed on the roof and seemed forlorn as Uncle George, aunt Edwina and velvet drove away into the evening sun. Velvet's friend continued to crane its neck in longing; long after the jeep had disappeared behind a clump of bushes.

Every week the family returned to the farm, but sometime Uncle George went alone. On every occasion he took Velvet who, on every occasion, found and brought his friend home. This happened for sometime, until, one day, Velvet's pal did not show up in the afternoon, nor the next day, nor the next, or the next. This continued as Velvet left in the morning but always returned at night and slept in his usual place on the roof.

Uncle George returned home with Velvet but did not visit the farm the next weekend. However, the next week uncle George returned with Velvet but left Rover home. In the morning Velvet went as usual and returned in the afternoon. That particular evening, however, Velvet did no sleep on the roof, but roosted on a beam inside the camp some height from the ground.

The next morning when uncle George awoke and had his breakfast, he took some corn in a calabash and offered it to Velvet.

Velvet turned his eyes to the calabash and started backing away as the corn was offered. As Velvet moved backwards, uncle George was forced to follow with his offering in his outstretched hand. Velvet backed until he reached a trail at the edge of the forest. Uncle George now realized that Velvet wanted him to follow, so he put the calabash down, and started behind Velvet who now went by small hops by flapping his wings.

They had gone a quarter of a mile into the forest when Velvet made a short flight and alighted on a low branch near the bole of a huge mora tree with two buttresses forming a V. There on a rough nest of leaves and sticks, sat Velvet's pal.

As uncle George cautiously approached the nest, he was astonished to behold half-naked chicks as the mother retreated some distance away.

Velvet flew down from his branch and waddled to uncle George and squatted at his feet, as if to say, "Are you not proud of your grand-children"?

(Below: the powis, *Black Currassow*, photo by Graham Watkins: Source: www.stabroknews.com)

****

The Waracabra That Wanted His Chicks to Sing Like A Quadrille

High up among the branches of a locust tree a quadrille wanted to build its nest. For two weeks now they had been gathering sticks to make a nest where a huge branch joined the main trunk. They lined the nest with the softest down materials that could have been found. This was gathered from the dried bark of the milkweed plant, which grew as secondary growth in the abandoned farmland.

Having finished, mama deposited two speckled brown eggs in the snug nest. Papa and Mama took turns incubating the eggs. As one went out to feed, the other will sit dolefully in the nest yet with alert eyes as each not only perused the tree-tops but also the brown ground and leaves below.

Between the buttresses of a nearby mora tree a pair of shiny waracabra had built their nest of sticks and lined it with feathers. Two grey-blue eggs were lovingly deposited in this crude yet comfortable nest.

It was just after the rains and there were ample amounts of seeds and nuts on the ground and myriads of insects that sometimes flew over the canopy to be caught by the waiting Passeriformes that station themselves in the upper branches for the purpose of satisfying their hunger.

Among the branches of the middle storey of the forest dwelt brilliant hummingbirds on their eternal quest for nectar among the dazzling orchids and flowers that festooned this stratum of the forest and perfumed the atmosphere with their sweet and indescribable fragrance.

As soon as the two eggs of the quadrille were hatched, mama quadrille and papa quadrille exclaimed almost simultaneously, "Are they not the most beautiful babies in the world"?

"Yes", assented papa quadrille to themselves, as he gazed at their two half-naked off-springs.

They were exceedingly happy, so much so that both mama and papa quadrille burst out into the most melodious notes spontaneously.

Well, everyone knows, that despite the drab color, the quadrille is, without saying, the most melodious warbler in all creation. Mama waracabra heard this music and was so enthralled with its quality that she seemed to fall in a trance.

When papa waracabra returned in the afternoon, mama said, "Papa, all this time we had been living near two of the greatest musicians ever".

"Is that so?" queried papa waracabra.

"Do papa, as soon as it is morning, ask them to sing for us. The beautiful music will do wonders for our un-born babies, and hearing such beautiful music in their earliest infancy, they may even learn to sing", said mama waracabra.

"If what you say is true", said papa, "then I shall ask them. This will do our babies all the good in the world. They might even learn to sing".

Just then papa quadrille burst forth with the most melodious tune. He was gazing at his little babies.

Papa waracabra on the ground looked up and remained speechless until papa quadrille paused. He flew up on a nearby branch.

"Hello, neighbor", he shouted at the top of his lungs. Qudrille heard. He paused and craned his small neck forward peering into the gloom under the tree.

"What can I do for you, sir? queried the quadrille.

"Oh neighbor, you have the most melodious voice in the world ...!"

"Thank you," replied quadrille.

"I was thinking", said the waracabra, "That is, my wife and I would like to ask you, since our babies are about to be hatched in a few days, we will appreciate if you can spare some of your valuable time to sing to them. We are sure that they will learn the tunes in their very infancy".

"Our days are very busy now since we have two extra mouths to feed", replied papa quadrille, and we have to look out for long tail in case he slithers up and eats our darlings".

"Oh, I can take care of that problem and give you extra time to look for food", replied papa waracabra. "You know that I hate long tail, and he is afraid of me. We are sworn enemies".

"All right", agreed papa waracabra. "If you will look out for long tail and protect my babies, I will sing to your babies, but only in the evenings".

"I gladly agree and I am sure my wife will appreciate it. I am going to tell her now".

The warcabra couple was overjoyed. "Our babies will learn to sing beautifully and also be the most beautiful birds in the world to live in the forest. Do you remember how maam envies our plumage?" mama waracabra asked.

"Powis and duroquarro and all the birds will envy us for having the most beautiful and also the most melodious off-springs in all the world", said papa.

Evening after evening papa quadrille flew down from his high perch and warbled and sang to the unhatched eggs. During mid-day hours both mama and papa quadrille flew off to collect insects to feed their fledglings who grew rapidly.

After some time some meek pe pee-ping were heard between the buttresses as the waracabra chicks emerged into the bright outside world. Mama and papa waracabra were overjoyed, anticipating the day when their off springs will start to sing like the quadrille. They brought the choicest and most nutritious seeds and insects that they could find for their young and fed them lovingly. They dropped the seeds and showed the chicks, pretending to be eating them, repeating the process until the chicks learnt to swallow them. The chicks rapidly aped and learnt to eat and this resulted in their rapid growth. Every evening uncle quadrille sang to them. They quickly grew into charming and beautiful chicks, shedding their baby down and putting on shiny mauve-grey feathers on their backs with the shiniest pale cream and soft black feathers on the rest of their bodies. Their beaks were the shiniest as if polished. The only feature that mama and papa did not like was the skinny legs.

By this time the quadrille chicks had left home for another part of the forest to grace it with their melodious tunes. Meanwhile the waracabra chicks started to say "Unc-goo, unc-goo, unc-goo ...".

Papa waracabra was overjoyed, since he told papa quadrille. "See, they already call you uncle. Soon they will start to sing. Teach them well".

Papa waracabra even went to the edge of the open savannah and even in the secondary growth of old farms, where he caught and piled up insects and caterpillars. He next filled his stomach with nuts and seeds, grabbed up the insects and caterpillars in his beak and took them to papa quadrille so he could give longer practice to his nephew and niece.

Mama waracabra and papa waracabra did all they could to encourage their babies to sing, but the most they got out of them was a lower sound, "Pak-goo, pak-goo, pak-goo". Try as they might, they could only mutter, "Pak-goo, pak-goo, pak-goo" and, sometimes, "pik-pik-pik", pik-pik-pik, in swift succession.

Uncle quadrille and his wife, discouraged in not being a successful teacher, flew away to sing their melodious tunes to other creatures. They never forgot the relationship until today, and kept always in touch; and so, when you hear a quadrille sing, there is always waracabra nearby.

And still, the waracabra remains the beauty on the ground and the quadrille the sweetest singer in the world.

(Above: left, The "quadrille" or Musician Wren. Source: www.en.wikipedia.org)
(Above: right, the "waracabra" or grey back trumpeter. Source: www.en.wikipedia.org)

****

Shea, The Enigmatic Princess of The Rupununi!

A few years ago after Im Thurn reached the Rupununi Savannahs, some adventurous individuals, long after, ventured forth and introduced the Texas longhorn to the area. Most of the itinerant cattle drovers returned to the Coastlands and civilization, while a few remained with the fledgling ranchers and generally wandered around captivated by the landscapes and the 'natives'.

One such drover, Henry, a fickle fellow, could not make up his mind whether to stay or to return to the comfort of urban life. This irresolution soon saw him wandering among the villages of the local population where he fell in love with an exquisitely beautiful slim golden maiden.

As custom demanded, he made this known to the maiden's father. His acceptance into the tribe and then the household occasioned a tribal meeting. It was agreed that he be accepted provided that he adhered to all the doctrines and customs of the tribe. One of the customs was, once a young man evinced love for a maiden, he moved in with the family and cut a field to show that he was capable of taking care of a family. This plot of land, however, formed part of the patrimony and, afterwards, had nothing to do with the courting couple.

Henry, the sailor who had jumped ship and seized the opportunity of driving cattle through dangerous humid and tropical jungle just for the mere adventure, was not used to wielding a machete, much less an axe; and so, after a short time after the novelty had worn off, he was so sore in body mind and spirit that, within the month, he had planned to escape that ordeal. The last evening when Henry and Volincia went down for the evening bath at the secluded part of the river, their love-making was ever more intense and passionate than before -- Henry, because he was aware that it was his last ever night with Volincia, and she, because she had now enamored herself fully with this tall fair skinned straw-colored hair demi-god.

Henry had planned his escape well. Nights before, in the guise of going night-fishing, he had purloined a store of tasso and farine from the camp of a family who had moved temporarily into the foothills for the purpose of cutting a field. This family had no bullock cart and saved themselves a daily commute by staying in a temporary camp on the site where they were cutting the field.

On his appointed night, Henry waited until he heard the snores from all the hammocks rising and falling with even timbre. He surreptitiously slid out of his hammock, sidled away from the open doorway and lost no time in putting as much distance between the benab and himself. He tucked the food under his arm and made his way directly to the corral of his erstwhile boss.

Henry selected the stallion he rode in with, assuring himself that the horse would be less skittish since it ought to remember him. Quietly he swung a simple saddle from a horizontal log of the corral on the horse's back and walked the animal about half-a-mile towards the entrance of the forest trail that would take him back to the distant Coastlands and civilization, and away from axe and machete. It was then at the edge of the forest that he mounted the stallion. Assuring himself that now no one would hear the hoofs of the horse he rode away into the stygian darkness trusting the instinct of his horse to transport him away from his ordeal.

Having about a six-hour head start, he knew that, by the time those who mattered, realized his intentions and likely path or action, pursuit would be useless. He thus concentrated all his will and effort to any future dangers he may encounter along the somber, humid and hot jungle trail.

At the stroke of dawn, when the matriarch awoke her daughter to stoke up the fire under the tuma pot, no one missed Henry. But when the father returned from his morning ablutions, he noticed the empty hammock and thought it strange since he did not pass the occupant neither to nor from the creek. No one was especially worried when Henry did not show up for early breakfast prior to going off to the field. It was thought that, since he did not catch any fish the previous night, he was gone to repair his fortune. When the neighbor came to report the loss of his horse in the evening, then it fully dawned on the populace of the whereabouts of Henry. This was quickly confirmed when some young men returned from the savannah trail that joined the forest.

The departure was accepted with mixed feelings among various members of the household, but none was as sad as Volincia at the loss of her beloved. For the entire week she did not sleep a wink, but went on with her chores as usual. However the discerning would have glanced the stoicism not in her eyes but a change in her entire demeanor. She went about like an automaton with a sad and faraway look.

Although her mother realized her daughter's agony, she did not, for one moment, broach the subject with her. Consoled and empathized with by family members seemed not to assuage, but to irritate her.

About a month passed and things went on in the usual way in the village. All seemed well.

Since Sunday was a day of rest, everybody slept late. For the first time in a month Volincia felt a little better as Henry's face became more faded in her mind. This morning she and her mother journeyed down to the creek to fetch some water for morning use. The mother felt well as she noticed the apparent change in her daughter. They filled their gourds, balanced them on top of the banks and waded into the stream to brush their teeth and scrape their tongues with the slender twigs they were chewing.

Suddenly Volincia seemed to stagger as from vertigo. The mother noticed and rushed towards her daughter and steadied her. Reflexively the daughter doubled over and started to retch uncontrollably. This lasted for a few minutes after she washed her mouth and drank some water when the vomiting started anew. Mother and daughter returned home, the mother in a very pensive mood and the daughter with sad and bleary eyes and an inflamed face.

This continued for some time and very shortly the entire village knew of Volincia's condition. Many did not openly discuss it with her, but their attitude, as they stood in close-headed groups and broke up as soon as she approached them, spoke volumes to her, which seemed to affirm the fact that they were discussing her and, perchance, avoiding her intentionally.

The whole village seemed to develop a strained relationship towards Volincia. She did not seem anymore to enjoy the easy camaraderie that once existed with her peers. It must be borne in mind that, among the tribe, family was a sacred institution and illegitimacy was frowned upon but accepted with great reluctance and reticence in some cases, because such practices were considered taboo.

As Volincia became larger and appeared to waddle as she moved about, a sort of fascination seemed to seize the bolder maidens whose friendship seemed to impart some sort of courage and strength to the erstwhile hapless maiden.

And since there would be no one to share in her pains when she went into labor, a hut was constructed in the downstream end of the village from where she carried out her domestic duties during her last moon. Volincia now shunned mixing with those who had recently befriended her, but found a small hidden niche on the opposite side of the bank of the river, which she claimed as her special hideout.

There secluded from prying eyes, she washed and bathed, and many a time sat on a comfortable rock dangling her feet in the coffee-colored water, reminiscing on her condition, and thinking what the future held for her.

One morning in early August, while thus engaged in the private reverie, she felt a stinging pain in the lower regions of her abdomen. Maternal instinct took over. She, there upon, hurried to her benab, lit a single oil lamp, spread her blanket and laid prostrate on the ground. Suddenly the pain became more excruciating; the pain became convulsions, which began coming nearer and nearer together. She seemed to blackout after one of these bouts during which a guttural groan escaped her lips as the baby made herself into the world.   A far away and distant cry seemed to bring back Volincia to reality and aroused her from her torpor. She came to realize that, between her loins all covered in blood, laid a tow-headed girl, all of about eight pounds, making crying sounds which increased louder and louder as seconds passed. After full realization dawned on her, Volincia got staggeringly up, took up her baby and wended her way to the stream and to her own private place where she washed the baby. She then cleaned herself with deliberation as she held the baby in one arm. She air-dried the now screaming infant and held her tiny mouth to one of her breasts, where the infant hungrily, presently clasped her lips and started to suckle.

The new mother now gingerly returned to the benab where she placed a clean and unused blanket in the hammock and climbed in with the baby. After the baby was swaddled in a specially made wrap for her, and having slaked her hunger, she seemed to have fallen asleep. The baby was placed in the hammock and gently rocked where it instantly fell asleep.

No smoke from her fire attracted the nearest neighbor who brought over some food as she suspected what had occurred. After the neighbor ascertained that her suspicions had been justified, she gently spoke to the new mother, gave her the food that she brought and asking that, when Volincia wanted anything, she had only to shout, she gently backed herself out of the benab, as was the custom during such occasions. The neighbor then took the news to Volincia's parents.

The father brought the Peiman who performed certain rites with fire and water, paying obeisance to the four winds and the sun, moon and earth, praying for the happy life of the infant and invoking the blessings of all for a long and prosperous life for mother and infant.

They now realized that the baby was an indescribably beautiful female infant sporting a full head of hair of a color never witnessed on anyone among the tribes. The color of the hair was a cross between flax-blond and a slight reddish brown. The skin of the infant was paler than any ever seen among the newborn before, and, as the grandparents looked in awe at its angelic face, it let out a feeble sound as if asking to be cuddled. The grandmother leaned over the hammock and, for the first time, whispered the child's secret name in her ear as given to her by the Peiman. The mother and the child only would know the name, as she grows older. The grandmother will never utter the name again. They then gave her the name of Shea by which name she will be known to all from then onwards. Shea's secret name will only be known to herself and her mother. This tradition of naming has been brought down since before their Great Trek from Pura, uncountable moons ago.

Shea became the pride and joy of her grandparents and, as she grew, became the favorite of the entire village.

Since the tribe was domiciled near one of the galleria forests through which one of the numerous streams ran across the savannah from the Roraima Formation, they had to commute to their fields in the foothills. There the land was extremely fertile.

The swidden agricultural practice ensured the fertility of the soil, but kept the occupants moving from plot to plot as one plot became exhausted and the others regenerated. The plots are systemically cultivated, reaped and abandoned.

Before the beginning of the rainy season, when the lakes and streams become low, enormous amounts of fish could be obtained from the lakes and streams, which become mere ponds and truncated rivulets.

At such times whole villages would leave their homes and their entire households would journey to the areas of plenty. They would pitch crude shelters and occupy all their time in catching, cooking, eating and preserving the bounty. Haimara and pacu, lukanani and hassar, and a number of other edible ones form the principal part of their catch. *(Below: The "hiamara" fish of Guyana. Source: www.totalfisherman.com)*

During this time too, water being scarce, the wild animals of the forests and savannahs will come to these water holes to slake their thirst. It is during this time that they could be easily taken, especially savannah deer, tapir, capybara, peccary and the giant anteater or barim. All these are edible and make a very welcome addition to fish and provisions.

The entire population would spend enough time to procure enough fish to last a long time, sometimes until the next season comes around. However, it must be noted that they only catch until concession is reached that there will be enough stock left to adequately stock the rivers for the next season.

The routine of the villages revolves around the cultivating of the fields in the foot-hills, making farine and tapioca along with cassava -bread in their semi-permanent farm huts, the forages of the hunting parties in the forests, fishing in the streams, sometimes poisoning the streams to make fishes comatose and then catching them. In effect the whole of the existence of these natives is geared towards procuring the basic necessities of life.

Ten dry and wet seasons passed, during which time, Shea and her mother enjoyed an unparalleled closeness with the tribe based on mutual love and admiration. Shea became a leader among her peers and even some children older than herself. She could not help but put up with more attention than she could readily handle and, many times, resorted to the bosom of her mother for solace.

Nevertheless life was idyllic and full of interest with the constant change in scenery, the salubrious savannah and mountain air, the mostly outdoor activities under the tropical sun tempered by the constant breezes blowing from the mountain blowing across the savannah, all contributed to a life of ease for a healthy child.

Shea was a graceful nymph of ten with long hair that changed color as light played among the tresses as she tossed her head. Sometimes her hair appeared one color and sometimes another as the sun played as the tresses were tossed and turned. Shea's arms and legs seemed to grow out of proportion to the rest of her body while the complexion of her body radiated a golden white aura. Her eyes were of a blue-green hue that defy accurate description, especially when she closed them then opened them after a moment of deep concentration. The flickering light of an evening savannah sun, as the clouds scudded across it, highlighted her beauty in ways that would have delighted a Raphael or Picasso. It seems that the entire gene pool from antediluvian times to Nordic aristocracy blended in mystic collusion with the biological inheritance of the maternal Mongolian legacy and extracted only the most beautiful and pleasing traits to fashion the physiognomy of this heavenly creature, this distinctive off-spring of Volincia.

During the eleventh year of her life, the entire family packed a few necessities with some food to go on the annual fishing trip. The two uncles, grandfather, grandmother, and mother and child set out one morning for their favorite spot on the bank of the lake. Since they left before dawn, before the sun peeped above the Ite palms, they were halfway there.

Suddenly, out of the adjoining forest, there emerged from some thick foliage two giant ant-bears and a baby ant-bear. This giant quadruped known as barim, but what the scientists call, (Myrmeccophaga tridactyla), is a long snouted, bushytailed, knuckle-walking mammal. The dark brown flesh is regarded as a delicacy among the inhabitants of the region. Her two stalwart brothers and her father readily advanced and warily circled the animals. It is well-known that if a barim gets to bear-hug a human, he may as well say farewell to his life. Local lore is rife where jaguars stalking barims quickly had the tables turned and, instead, ended up the victim. However, before the brothers had dispatched the huge male with lance arrow and machete, the women folk had caught up with them. Shea was in time to witness the last blows, and saw the large amount of crimson blood that gushed forth from the throat wounds curving like half-moons. She turned her face with nauseating abhorrence and emptied her morning meal all over the savannah grass.

Having butchered the meat and sharing it among the various warashis, they continued without further incident towards the lake and pitched their tent early in the post noon.

Shea skipped her evening meal, pleading nausea. Later on she ate a little farine and drank a bit of tapioca porridge. Unknowing to anyone, Shea, having witnessed the slaughter and demise of the barim, was so upset by the experience that she vowed in her pre-teen mind to cease forever the consumption of all animals.

Although she helped with the cleaning, gutting, and drying of the fish she ate nothing but vegetables.

When they eventually returned to the village, everyone seemed to be aware of the withdrawn mood of their princess. Shea became pensive and melancholy and, much of the time, remained uncommunicative. She started to pine away and lose much of her aura. Gone were the cool vitality and cool and endless vigor she exhibited when playing. She now shunned the play-square and more and more courted companionship and solace of her hammock.

The grandparents summoned the Peiman, who on the last day of the full moon, started a purification process. This necessitated that he goes into a trance and consult with, and be advised by, the Good Spirits. Having performed various rites and rituals and the casting of various articles from his sacred bag, he woke from the trance.

The Peiman advised that, in order for Shea to recapture her former vivacity and health, she had to leave the savannah country and live in the mountains. She must forswear village life for one of in isolation for many years.

After the Peiman had left, it was decided that the family must do as advised. However, the two uncles and the mother would remain in the village to tend the family's vast fields, while the grand parents would accompany Shea and, regardless of how long it took, would only return when she is completely cured of her malady.

The farewell was sad indeed as the trio left for the mountains. After a week they reached a spot in the mountains foretold by the Peiman. The family settled in, cut a small field and embraced a life of austerity. From the very first day, Shea felt that some invisible force was beckoning her and so she wandered off into the forest alone. The grandparents, concerned about her safety, secretly followed her only to discover Shea under a huge locust tree gently stroking the flanks of a huge jaguar, while saucer-sized morpho butterflies were flitting around and even lighting on her outstretched

hand.

(Above: A morpho butterfly. Source: www.en.wikipedia.org)

The grandparents, although petrified, nevertheless discovered an inner peace in this tense situation and withdrew less they desecrate the sanctity of the moment with their presence. From then onwards, the grandparents never feared for Shea's safety.

Days passed, then months lengthened into years during which time the grandparents secretly watched Shea's communication with every sort of forest creature. They soon lost their fear or apprehension of any harm befalling their grandchild.

One day Shea appeared out of the forest in a brand-new gossamer outfit made out of a material unknown to anyone. It was shiny and smooth and seamless, and seemed to fit her as another skin. When questioned she only shrugged and made indecipherable gestures. By this time Shea had already regained her vitality and aura, although she seemed not to eat anything. She was the picture of youth and health. When they suggested that they return home she pleaded for a little more time to cavort with her friends. Since they could not refuse her anything, they always acceded to her demands.

Sad was the day when the grandmother died. The grandmother and grandfather had embraced the vegetarian way of life. Things seem to go on as usual until one day on her return from the forest her keen nostrils detected the odor of cooked flesh. From that day onwards, a gulf seemed to separate granddaughter and grandfather.

As this gulf grew wider and wider, Shea spent more and more time from her grandfather's dwelling. Sometimes she stayed away weeks on end.

Did the duo return to civilization? Certainly not! We heard of Shea some years later when she became the heroine of W H Hudson's - *"Green Mansions"*.

The Grandfather! It is hoped that he is resting in the big benab in the sky happily re-united with his faithful wife.

****

The Last Arawak Of Hyawa

Adourie and his wife were under the fugrocop tree feasting on the sweetly tart yellow flesh of the fruits that dropped on the leaf-covered ground. Ever so often the wind penetrated the forest canopy and wafted among the slender branches and the semi-loosely-hung fruits will leave their precarious hold on the stems and plummet straight down as if aimed by an unseen hand.

Very often, as fresh fruits fell, Adourie and his wife will dart to the spot to eat as much as they could and as fast as they could. They knew from their experience that, once the morning grew older other occupants of the forest would be attracted by the sweet scent of the fruits and, that fast on the heels of these other foragers would come brother Jaguar. If the feeders failed to detect his stealthy approach, one or more of them will easily fall prey to his voracious appetite. It was thus that Adourie lost one of his wives.

Conveniently, nearby ran the dark amber waters of a cool mountain stream. As the waters flow babblingly among the embedded stones and the ancient tacoubas, kuti, dari, kabrishi, and other fishes with exotic names, swam in contented laziness as they occasionally darted from the dark recesses to capture a careless minnow that might haplessly have strayed into deep water. Sometimes too, these fishes gained sustenance from an unsuspecting dragonfly that might alight on the water or from some injured one that had fallen on the bosom of the stream.

From this stream all the animals slaked their thirst after having fed on the tart fugrocop berries. Even brother Aroa sometimes satisfied his thirst from this source.

(Above: one of the psittacine birds – the parrot/parakeet family – www.en.wikipedia.org)

Above, over the verdant canopy, psittacine birds gave vent with their cries as they winged their way to their feeding grounds, composed in the thought of their young ones snugly asleep in their lofty nests.

Five miles down the Yuruan joined with its bigger cousin at the confluence at the junction known as the Dorado. At this confluence stood a lonely, newly constructed, hut. Its newly constructed state was still evident in the brown-green nature of the thatch. At this very early time in the morning, smoke was seeping through this thatch roof like a carelessly pulled boll of cotton, but, as it rose, it re-united into one into a thin straight column. When this column moved to the height of the surrounding trees, it assumed a corkscrew pattern only to dissipate as it reached the sunshine filtering above.

In this hut with its spartan furnishings of a fireplace made of three stones, a crudely constructed bench and table to one side, was slung a tibisiri hammock. The floor was sand and the walls were made of the bark of the baramalli tree. In this hammock, lazily swinging from side to side, sat a half-clad bronze giant of a man, his feet inches from the ground as he passively cogitated on the fate that has propelled him into this self-imposed loneliness.

One moon ago, returning from the hunt, Simara had found his hut burnt to the ground with some household articles strewn helter-skelter outside in the yard.

He slowly and cautiously withdrew from the clearing trying to pick up some sign of what had transpired in his absence. What of his wife, infant son and two teen-age daughters? He still had his warishi on his back as he circled ever nearer and nearer to detect some clue as to the fate of his family.

Suddenly with a loud twang an arrow embedded itself in his warishi. Only the thick slab of dried meat in which the arrow now quivered saved his life.

Quick as a flash Simara fell to the ground. He was careful, however, to fall on his side across the path with his face in the direction from whence the arrow came. His hand was stretched over his head in the sparse undergrowth, the bow and a single arrow clutched in the other hand, as he opened one eye and very cautiously peered around for the slightest movement.

Simara's mind started to wander, as he lay prone on the comforting bosom of the earth, feeling naked to his soul. He bitterly recalled that, because of these same raids by the Caribs, that he had left the main tribe and settled at this fertile place that he named Hyawa, after the tree that issued a pungent gum by that name that he found growing there. He felt that the enemies were easily attracted to villages where there were more women and booty.

Simara silently rued the day when he left the main tribe and forsook safety in numbers. He now had nothing to show for his foolhardiness and, now, he faced certain death if his assailants were still watching him. He recalled that he had been safe for five years as, "Every year the Caribs from all quarters gathered round the Arawaks... and attacked them". He could not now repair this damage and return to the tribe. Even if he did, what would be the use since he was proved wrong and has no asset that will assist him to inveigle himself again into the good graces of the tribe?

As he lay vulnerably thus, every sinew and sense alert for the slightest sound or movement, a heavy sadness crept over him. A sense of dejection permeated his being and he started to shiver uncontrollably, despite the dank humidity of the atmosphere. He soon realized that the shivering would have attracted anyone if he were still being watched.

He arose, throwing caution to the winds. He involuntarily let a low moan escape his lips as his heart swelled with sadness. A passion came over him and silent tears escaped down both cheeks and blinded him. He started walking slowly at first until he increased his rate to a steady trot. His mind became as blank as all he could remember was the slanting rays of the sun over his shoulder.

It was already dark when Simara slipped over a fallen log and lay face down in the damp pegasse. His exhausted body refused to stir. He did not care to live, and hence refused to get up. He soon fell into an exhausted and dreamless sleep.

The distant sound of a maipuri feeding noisily on fallen ite seeds slowly penetrated his torpid mind. He awoke slowly as his limbs ached in every joint. Memory slowly returned to his tortured brain as his limbs started responding to his will. He slowly and painfully got up, gazing at the deep imprint that his face made in the pegasse.

(Above: the tapir Source: www.stabroeknews.com)

While he sat on the decaying log, the undergrowth started to brighten as Sol ascended the Heavens and sent its lancing rays penetrating the forest undergrowth. In complete contrast to the surroundings, Simara's heart weighed heavily in his chest. The sadness of the twelve hours of the day before returned ten-fold as he took stock of his predicament.

He, Simara, always had a keen mind an outstanding ken for survival. He dearly loved his family and fondly looked forward to the day when his beautiful daughters would need husbands and thus enlarge his household.

In the throes of the depression of his spirit, he lost all hopes of ever seeing his beloved family again. As the pain mounted in his breast, he swore a great oath to avenge his family regardless of how long it took. A guttural growl arose from his bowels with pain, made its way up to his stomach, and finally through his throat and out his mouth with a great feral ferocity.

After this a sense of realism returned. He deliberately calmed his innermost turmoil by taking several deep breaths. Now with a more sedate composure, he rose, walked away from the place he considered bed, went some way into the underbrush, made a fox-hole and attended to his excretory needs.

When Simara returned to his warishi, something scurried away as he approached. It was a porcupine that had taken out a sizeable bite out of the shoulder of the peccary. The sweet smell of the roasted meat reminded Simara of his corporeal needs. He however ignored this and shouldered his warishi and journeyed until he met a wide coffee colored stream. As he dropped his warishi and slaked his thirst, several blow-flies, attracted by the odor of the meat, alighted on the open top portion. On returning he shooed them away, made a fire, cut a thick slab from where the rodent had bitten, roasted it, and devoured it with relish. He made the fire bigger and re-smoked the remaining portions, then returned the entire portions to his warishi where he strapped them well and continued to walk along the side of the stream. It was thus that, late that afternoon, he came to the confluence of the Yuruan and the Supamo. The area seemed isolated enough, so he quickly erected a powis-tail, since it was already getting late, made a fire, ate a piece of the smoked meat and bedded down for the night in his hammock swung between a sapling and a firmly bedded down stake planted at an acute angle to the surface.

For the second night in a row Simara did not dream. But, before he slept, he took a very keen note of the wild-life of the area; maam-swa in numbers, whistling to their mates, the noisy marudi in the touroniro trees feasting on the green berries, the cooing of the doves and pigeons, the call of numerous familiar edible fauna, but, especially the numerous calls attracted his attention and kept him listening until he fell into an exhausted sleep. The Arrow, referring to himself by his nickname, Simara did not wake or dream during the entire night. Although all these creatures are diurnal, most of them call regularly in the nights, but especially in the early evenings and pre-dawn periods.

He woke very early in the morning and made a breakfast of broiled ham and turu tea. (He had selected a turu palm that had ripe fruits to cut down to get leaves for his powis tail, so he also got the fruits).

After reconnoitering the area, he decided that he was at the best spot to erect a permanent home. He was on a triangle protected on two sides by the river, the land was high and dry, and there were numerous hardwood trees suitable for erecting a suitable domicile. He had also passed some abandoned fields so getting planting materials would be easy.

He remained, in the meanwhile, in his powis tail and started cutting a field for planting. All building materials he encountered were carefully measured, trimmed, peeled and stored for building. These he took to the place where he had decided to build his home and stacked them in sorted piles. As the field was drying he went to an abandoned farm and returned with a number of dried gourds, which he cleaned and made into water utensils and other storage receptacles. He also brought some undeveloped vegetables and lengths of sugar cane. Within two weeks of his arrival he had finished building his benab and shaped a huge yellow silverballi log into the contours of a corial. His meat was now nearly exhausted. He sat in the hammock with his foot barely off the sandy floor. Soon, the hammock was swinging as regular as a pendulum. He thought of how his ancestors had once defeated his deadly enemies, the fierce Meyanow tribe who used to devastate their villages regularly. Simara now recalled how many times they had defeated the cannibalistic Caribs by stratagem, and of his leaving the tribe with his family and living alone in Hyawa. The thoughts of his family returned to his mind, but rather than dwell on this, he decided that, since it was early morning, he would go in search of meat to replenish his larder.

He wended his way silently along the bank and, to his delight, found the fugrocop tree. He told himself that he was extremely lucky to find a tree fully laden with fruit so near from home.

He was refreshing himself with some of the fruits and, at the same time, was on the lookout for some of the denizens that might have the same idea of refreshing themselves early.

No sooner than he straightened up that he noticed, from the corner of his eye, some movements. The animals seemed to have sensed his presence and kept their distance.

About twenty yards from the fruiting fugrocop was the huge bole of a tree, the leaves of which looked like scales, so great they were from the ground. About seven feet up this bole was a huge vine, as thick as a man's thigh, encircling the trunk in a loop. Simara mounted on this comfortable perch, and sat silently surveying his surroundings. Although he saw numerous animals, acouri and adouri and even a big-eyed buck some distance away, he could not understand why they were not approaching the tartly luscious fruits that are directly under the tree.

Suddenly, in a sparse thicket to his right, he discovered a furtive movement out of the corner of his eye. He slowly turned to face the direction when he espied a huge jaguar crouched on its haunches with its tail spasmodically twitching. Simara looked brother Aroa straight in the eyes. Aroa slowly yawned displaying its yellow fangs as he simultaneously passed his left paw across his face. Now Simara understood why the animals were so skittish.

Simara fixed a poisoned arrow to his bow, drew the bowstring to his right ear and sent the shaft straight under the left shoulder into the great carnivore's heart. With a thunderous roar the huge cat sprang towards Simara, but only succeeded at landing at the foot of the great tree, where, after a few twitches, it lay still in death.

Simara descended from his perch and bent over the great feline to extract his arrow buried to the heart of the great beast. He only had time to turn. With a thunderous roar as if from nowhere, a great male cat sprang, with legs set wide, and gaping thunderous jaws. As if in slow motion Simara put up his hands to ward off the great carnivore. Both arms were instantly crushed between the great jaws like matchsticks as the huge left claws, with their great retractile claws, severed Simira's jugular vein like so much tissue paper. In the same instant Simara's life gushed out in frothing bursts, saturating the leached soil in the process.

Attracted by the hubbub, a canoe of returning hunters from the Yuruan jumped ashore and discovered what was taking place. The huge male cat with every sinew alert, and with its forelegs astride Simara's torso, seemed to sense the men. He turned towards them and with a spit and a bark slinked away before any of them could even fit an arrow to his bowstring.

Great was the surprise when the men found brother Aroa's victim was a fellow human, and greater still, when they found the dead female jaguar nearby.

The mutilated body was placed in a corial while two men started to retrace the faint steps of the victim. More for courage than for direction the two on land shouted for the boaters at short intervals to maintain contact.

After about two and half hours the men on land arrived at Simara's newly constructed camp. They read all the signs to reconstruct the drama that has caused this unlikely encounter.

Then giving Simara a decent burial by burning his camp over him a few of the men decided to stay after noticing the newly cut field. Most of all they noticed the strategic location as being suitable indeed for further settlement. Suitable and fertile land constituted the broad expanse of the triangle with a backdrop of steep mountains, while on the two sides the rivers formed a natural and easily defended boundaries if the occasion ever arises.

They found out where Simara was by retracing his footsteps to his old burnt out benab at Hyawa. It was an open secret among the Arawaks of the behavioral idiosyncrasies of the "Arrow Who Liked To Live Alone."

Hyawa was burnt to dust. Simara was dead. His wife and family were unaccounted for or were among strange people. The last of his blood was now in the intestines of ants and other vermin of the forest floor. Perchance the next season's fugrocop will ripen with a brownish red, having fed on the life-blood of one who only sought safety and solitude. Such a one is gone, but in the natural order of things, this is just a phase. Perhaps his life is with Manitou, looking down on the frailties of human kind, or perhaps his soul is in the seed of a womb in a great metropolitan city to a brave future against everything he stood for in this phase, in the unending cycle of birth and rebirth.

(Above: the "whitie" fruit. Source: www.TnTisland.com)

****

The First Green Macaw

For two seasons now, Kona had been watching an odd sight. Early every morning, exactly over his benab, high over the mora and other timber trees, flew a flock of macaws in strict pairs to their feeding grounds. Raucous cries always heralded their passing in the early morning with the golden sun reflecting from their plumage although this sun did not yet reach the lower elevations. It was heartening to watch in the early morning.

What was noticeable, however, was that last year's leaders had taken up secondary positions as if allowing the youngsters the opportunity to lead. The discerning can recognize this by the slight difference in their coloration, which can be readily noticeable.

Kona knew this since he noticed an odd pair in the formation just after the May-June rainy season. He had discovered this anomaly just behind the leading pair. This one macaw was distinctly blue whilst the other one was of the red and yellow variety, like the rest of the flock.

Kona was first attracted to this flock of birds, not because he happened to see the odd pair, but because, since he visited his elder brother's Kanko's village, his little daughter, Tani, was yearning to have a pet macaw of her own. All the cousins boasted of their own tame pets as they went around their chores and games. Tomo had his abouya that dogged his heels whenever he went anywhere. Milti had her pet Toco that rode on her shoulder whenever she went to the creek to fetch water. Even little Piko had his pet Adouri, which, not yet tame, was kept in a cage and fed with nuts and fruits.

After they returned from a visit to Kanko's village, Kona resolved that he would get a pet for his daughter, a pet that would be the envy of everyone. Probably that was why, at the rising of the sun each morning, he waited in the clearing of his yard, peering upward and straining his ears to await the passing of the macaws. His eyes followed the birds as soon as they appeared above the wall of the vertical trees and followed them westwards until they disappeared. It was because of this that he observed that the odd-pair took over the lead of the flock. At first he thought that the leading pair had somehow died, but he thought it unlikely that both male and female would meet their demise simultaneously. He reverted to counting them. Great was his joy when he found all ten pairs noisily winging their way towards the west with their long tails pointing towards the morning sun.

Kona surmised that something must have happened for the alpha pair to surrender its position to the odd couple, but think as he might, he could no come up with a plausible explanation. One afternoon he saw the great Blue, as he had now come to designate the leader, with food in its bill flying back from whence they came. Now everyone knows that this was a sure sign that the pair had recently become parents. This, he thought to himself, must have caused the pair to become leaders. "Is parenthood a qualification for leadership!" he asked himself. If this was so, then the flock must be composed of mainly young birds. Since more or less all of the flock must have been of diverse ages, this left him in a deeper quandary. He had another haunch, and so decided to find the nesting place of the newly minted family. So, the next afternoon he told his eldest nephew that they would embark on a journey.

That afternoon they packed some provisions for a few days in a warishi and left it at the entrance of the benab. That morning Kona noted the exact direction from which the flock came, even noting the exact branch on the mora tree over which they flew on the eastern side, and the spire of the giant cokerite tree, which gave him the exact bearing as to the path of the birds' flight and the direction in which they travelled.

They took up the warshi and left the farm early after lunch the next day, Kano taking the old arakapoosa and the nephew taking his machete. The arakapoosa was sparingly used because of a lack of powder and balls; but who knows what they may encounter, or how far they had to go.

Through the afternoon they travelled, making a beeline in the direction they wanted to go. They stopped early in the afternoon and pitched temporary camp to await the return of the birds and assured themselves that they were going in the right direction. Presently, a distant cry was heard and the flock flew directly overhead.

The next morning, as soon as the flock passed, the two men started making tracks in the opposite direction from which the birds had come.

Late that same afternoon, they found themselves at the edge of a fair-sized savannah, studded with ite palm trees in all stages of growth. There were clumps of young trees among older ones while others stood tall, over fifty feet, above the surrounding swamps with feathery fronds adorning the tops; some others again had died and stood without leaves like great stilts planted by some antediluvian giant.

As Kona and his nephew were taking in the scenery and preparing to pitch camp for the night beside the swamp, as from afar came the sound of the approaching birds. No sooner than they were heard when the entire flock dipped lower. The leading pair flew directly to one of the dead palms and was lost behind the great trunk. One had some kind of fruit in its beak while the rest made their way and alighted on the tall trees that bordered the swamp.

About twenty minutes later, the great Blue flew off to the adjoining trees while the mother that took the fruit that was left to cuddle the chicks. There was an opening about thirty feet up through which the mother entered the hollow tree. Kona and his nephew hastily made their crude shelters, slung their hammocks, had a cold dinner and bedded down as soon as it became dark. They made no fire so as not to alarm the birds.

Their plan was to harmlessly retrieve the chick/s from the nest. Anyone familiar with dead palm trunks, especially ite trunks, will be very familiar with the fact that, that apart from being very difficult to climb because of its smoothness and girth, knows that, invariably, that, in the old broken trees, the pith in the trunk readily disintegrates as soon as the tree dies. It gets very porous and can collapse within the trunk very easily. No one in his right senses will risk such uncertainties by climbing it.

The chicks must be retrieved in two ways. If the pith is rotten throughout the entire length of the trunk, then a wide hole is cut near the base of the trunk and, with the back of an axe or other heavy material, the trunk is hit very hard, in which case the entire nest will slowly descend as the tree is shocked. The chicks are now easily retrieved. However, if the pith of the trunk is not sufficiently rotten, then the trunk has to be felled, which, in some cases, might result in the death of the chicks, or recovering them severely traumatized. The former method is preferable but not always possible.

The next morning, just under the tonal volume of the howling baboons, the flock rose from their leafy abodes, as one started to circle the trunk with the nest, as if all of them were saying farewell for the day. The mother joined the flock that continued circling the trunk while papa took a peek inside. After this the entire flock rose into the air and winged its way westwards.

Kona and nephew rose and, after eating breakfast, they copiously rubbed one another's bodies with the oil of the crab-wood tree. They entered the water and wended their way to the trunk with the nest in it. With the back of the machete they sounded the trunk.

They were in luck. The tree sounded hollow down to the bottom. With some difficulty they cut a large hole in the trunk some distance from the bottom, on ascertaining that the entire trunk was hollow. They stuffed some savannah grass at the bottom to cushion the fall of the nest.

The nephew returned to the campsite and cut a manageable piece of wood with which to hit the trunk. The vibration, they hoped, would serve to bring down the descent of the nest towards the hole at the bottom, where the chicks will be easily retrieved.

(Above: colorful macaw in hole in ite tree trunk: Source: www.stabroeknews.com)

No sooner had they commenced to hit the trunk than down slid the nest. It rested on the bed of grass, displaying a single naked chick with large bulging eyes and an over-sized grey-green beak.

The men were overjoyed, but at the same time, a bit disappointed that the nest contained only one chick. They, however, tenderly removed it from the cozy nest. The nephew took off his shirt and wrapped it around the trembling chick. They returned to their makeshift camp, retrieved their scanty belongings, then the nephew plaited a broad-bottomed darwan and prepared to journey home.

The duo reached their village in the afternoon. In fact, although they did not see the macaws returning in the afternoon, they heard them and wondered what the parents would think when they discovered their offspring missing.

All the three families of the benabs, which composed of the village, were present to view and welcome the new arrival. Everyone was making comments of how big the chick was when Tani remarked that its eyes were as big as the eyes of Toma's abouya.

Since the eyes seemed as big as an abouya's, they all decided that it would be called Chaunco, (which is another name for the wild pig or peccary).

Tani took on full time care of Chaunco. Great was their surprise that, when it started growing feathers, they were not of the vivid blue of the father's nor the red and yellow of the mother. This fantastic bird grew a thick batch of feathers of vivid green, like the young leaves of the kakarali tree just after it had flowered.

At first everyone thought that Chaunco was a parrot fed by macaws by mistake, while some felt that Kona had played a trick on the inhabitants of the village. But as Chanco grew, it left no doubt that it was a macaw. It grew into the largest macaw seen by anyone. It seemed even bigger than the great Blue with tail feathers measuring nearly a full yard.

Upon close examination some dark blue feathers were seen intermixed on its back, which gave it a teal hue, while a few yellow and red feathers adorned the forward joints of both wings.

Chaunco became the favorite of all. She seemed so bonded with Tani sometimes a sad expectancy could be detected, which seemed to cloud its countenance if Tani came late from school.

When Tani reached the Fourth Standard she was awarded a scholarship at the High School at St. Ignatius. She took Chaunco and took care of it whenever this was required. The bird soon became a great favorite with all at the hostel.

At the end four years, Tani did so well that she was afforded an opportunity to study for the Advanced General Certificate of Education in the capital city of Georgetown. Chaunco travelled with her and readily became a favorite with the family where Tani spent her time.

During this time Tani's father died, having been infected with tetanus on a hunting trip when he was injured. This caused her mother to live with relatives who treated her, at most, casually. So when Tani passed her examinations with the highest grades and was offered an overseas scholarship to study medicine, she confided her dilemma to her only city friend, the Curator of the Zoological Park in the City.

Tani had frequently visited the zoo to study in its classroom. She also took Chaunco to be with animals of its own kind. Mr. Singh, the Curator, even offered Tani an exorbitant sum if she would sell her pet to the zoo, but she always refused. So, when she was offered the scholarship, she thought it best that Chaunco be afforded the opportunity to spend the time of absence of its mistress among its own kind.

Such a rarity soon attracted ornithologists from far and near. There was never a visitor to the zoo who failed to marvel at such a macaw, different from all the rest. Some scientists even attempted to collect specimens of blood to study, but in keeping with the promise to Tani, the Curator disallowed all such attempts.

For the last time, as Tani backed away from the gates of the park the Sunday afternoon prior to her leaving for overseas on Monday, two big tears rolled down both cheeks and stained her white blouse like the two big eyes of an abouya.

****

147

Why The Caiman's Skin Is Rough

Very, very, long ago when all beings, whether living in the heavens, or on earth, or under water, were required to gather their own food, all of them had their own peculiar way of obtaining their food honestly.

Tapir, when he was hungry, used to rub his great bulk on the trunks of trees and shake them. This caused the ripe fruits to fall. When the fruits fell, tapir will satisfy his hunger.

The bushmaster, being a carnivore, will gather souari nuts and hide them in little heaps. When acouri came to feed on these nuts bushmaster will pounce, fasten his fangs on the hapless victim and soon make a meal of it.

Fling-far (camoodi), on the other hand, will lay silently alongside a tacouba in the creek and, when a deer or other animal happen to venture near or go down to the creek to slake its thirst, the camoodie will either grab it with open jaws or throw its tail around the hapless victim, wrap around and squeeze and roll until it is asphyxiated, and camoodie will then unhinge its jaws and then make a meal out of it.

There was co-operation among some animals like the parrot and the labba, although the parrot was diurnal and the labba nocturnal. Parrot will only eat the succulent parts of the fruits and leave the nutty seeds, which labba will enjoy to its heart's content later. Sometimes if the seeds were very hard and labba could not get at the nuts, parrot will even leave some flesh on the seeds for labba to enjoy.

There was even co-operation between heavenly bodies and terrestrial beings. So that, when rains failed to come to the grass, the stars that like to see their pale light reflect with luminescence, among the blades of waving verdant grass, would weep and so provide dew to refresh the stalks and sparkle on the tips of every blade in the slanting rays of the morning sun.

It must be noted, however, that during this time, because it was so very long ago, many of the animals (and even the plants) were not exactly as we know them today. For example, the savannah grass was not the tough bunch grass that we know them today. They were long, slender, tender, graceful, and very succulent. The young of the deer and the tapir had no stripes, since there was no need for camouflage. Kiskadee was not yet then compelled to wear the bandage round its head, nor was the throat of marudi red.

The landscape was also different. The waterfalls were more spectacular. The flowers of the myriads of trees were much more colorful. The bimiti (Humming-birds), were more plentiful and the moss, with which they built their nests over streams to tell the next flood, grew on the crotch of every sapodilla tree. Even the echo of the call of the various birds carried farther and resounded with greater clarity than they now do.

Men never had to work so hard. They had not yet acquired the acquisitive trait of greed. Everything that they needed was at hand. They took and used to satisfy only their immediate wants, assured in the fact that to-morrow will provide for itself. So they always left the remainder so that others might have.

It was a time too, that, with few exceptions, the night animals knew only the night animals and the diurnal ones knew their kind. This did not mean that some did not encounter others. The twilight dwellers knew some of both worlds. There was even then communication between the flora and the fauna, and everything was in order. However, the different breeds of animals were not so diverse. There was one kind of aguti, one kind of tapir, one kind of kaiman and one kind of capybara too. Even the people were only one kind.

It goes without telling then that because things were so arranged, each would use its own time, and would not infringe on the rights of another. Waneeka, the Moon and Ya the Sun, even agreed to come down to the forests; Waneeka came only during the nights whenever its stomach was so empty as nearly to reach its back, and Ya, whenever it flared especially hard, lost a lot of energy.

No one ever stole another's food or reaped the fruits of another's labor. However, one day, one of the People found a huge monkey-pot fruit propped in the bole of a tree. Brother Hurwe had left it there the day before. When Brother Hurwe went the next day to fetch the sweet fruit for his pregnant wife, he found the hiding place empty. Try as he might he could not discover who committed such a dastardly and unprecedented act. So it happened that Brother Man, inadvertently, committed the first evil act. This state of affairs has continued to the present time, especially among men and lower species, like the rat and the hyena that would steal when no one was watching. Even some aquatic brothers who had very little dealing with people acquired this habit of purloining the fruits of one and another's labor.

This happened very gradually among some animals while with others it caught on quickly. For example, when the tribe of brother otter is hunting as a team, the fish is usually stored near the stream between the buttresses of a convenient tree. The team leaves one of their kind to guard the catch while the others continue hunting. Ever so often otters will steal the fish from man-made weirs and so rob the makers of the dam. Usually when Brother Man was ready to collect the fish, his stream would be devoid of any. So too, Brother Aguti had developed the habit of robbing Brother Man's farm. He would cleverly put his ear to the ground and tap it to obtain differential sound, which tells him where to dig to find ground provisions, which he liked, especially cassava. When he presently locates one, he will eat voraciously with one eye out for Brother Man.

During this time, Brother Caiman was of one breed only; of middle size, with a beautiful smooth skin that was the envy of other scaled reptiles. His skin glowed in the changing light of the water and attracted fishes to him, which were then easily caught. This made for a leisurely existence, which made Brother Caiman lazy, and then lazier, and lethargic as time went by. This caused him to develop two distinct qualities as time went by; one malign and one benign. The malign quality was that Brother caiman became lazier and lazier as time went by. So he made stealing a way of life. He raided the traps of the people. He raided the rivers dammed by The Planets and once even attempted to chase the Otter Watch away so he could feast on the fish. The watch's shrill alarm however summoned the rest of the tribe and Brother caiman barely escaped with his life.

(Above: caiman with crab in its mouth. Source: www.phillanoue.com)

The benign part of Brother Caiman's leisurely existence caused a slowdown in his metabolism to such an extent that he was only required to eat once a week. This made foraging less and less hectic. This also left him with a habit of seeking the easiest way of obtaining food: to wit raiding other people's traps and weirs.

Sometimes, to pep up his appetite, he will travel long distances over the land from stream to stream, where he knew that he could easily steal with the least bit of detection or effort.

One day Father Ya sent out an especially great flare and became very hungry. When everyone was retired for the night, he stayed up late and built a dam across the Arabapo river so that he could catch some fish when he awoke in the morning. Everyone is well aware of the abundance of this particular watercourse. Before morning, as would be expected, Father Ya sent his good friend Coatimundi to check the amount of fish trapped. Coati was very disappointed to find no fish, not even a solitary piaab.

The water, however, was muddy from the recent predation, but no tracks could be found because of the stony nature of the ground. However, Coati reported the situation to Father Ya. He was told to keep a keen look-out for any sort of theft since the stream would teem with an abundance once the dam is loosened and the river left to flow again and replenish itself'

Coati hid in a hollow mora log and slept for the better part of the day. Dusk came early to the river as the great Roraima Escarpment cast huge shadows over the forest. Coati awoke and started his vigil from the secret recess where he was ensconced. By and by a soft rustling heralded the entrance of an intruder. With a silent splash Caiman slid into the water. No sooner had he done this when he trapped a haimara in a little itabu on the side of the river. He soon had this scaly delicacy between his strong jaws.

He closed his eyes as he munched on his delicious and succulent repast. Coati slipped out of his hiding place and, with his belly close to the ground, slithered to the side of the stream. When he was directly in front Caiman, he rose to his full three feet on his back legs and looked straight into Caiman's eyes. Caiman was so engrossed and delighted with his juicy morsel in his mouth that his eyes were closed; but, as he opened them, the full focus of Ya's sentry slowly registered on his fuzzy brain. His bottom jaw dropped spilling the scraps that were still in his mouth.

Caiman was so shocked that, for a moment, he was completely paralyzed. He slowly crept up the bank and kept as low to the ground as he could and started pleading with the irate Coati. By this time two of Ya's messengers had two strong neebee ropes around Caiman's throat and tail, which rendered him completely immobile. In this piteous and forlorn condition, Caiman looked as if he could not harm a fly, much less rob the trap of the mighty. Caiman begged and pleaded and begged and pleaded until Ya took pity on him. However, all agreed that some form of punishment must be meted out to him as an example so that others may not harbor the least thought of stealing.

So, Ya ordered that Caiman must be given a beating. The guards were not to use their proper war clubs but a lighter and softer version from a different kind of tree but not the purple-heart as was their custom.

The guards commenced their task with gusto. They beat Caiman so much that they tanned his hide. His former opalescent hue was transformed to being black and blue all over. Great welts were raised all over his body. The skin, especially along the tail, was tattered on the top and swollen at the bottom.

Ya looked down from the firmament and spoke to Caiman. "Let this be a lesson to you, Caiman, forever. When you finally heal, your body will always retain the welts. Your skin will be tough as leather. Your tail will forever remain tattered as a reminder of your sin".

 "Thank you for my life Mighty One. I will try never to commit such acts in the future".

"One last thing", said Ya. "From now on, and for all times, all your children and children's children shall continue to bear your scars. One other thing, you shall never remain one tribe again. Some of your children will become pygmies wearing spectacles, some of them will become black and overgrown and lazy, and some of them will have teeth sticking out of the corners of their mouth, as you have now, from the beating. The rest will remain as you are.

Ya so cursed caiman, and so it remained ever after; four bumpy tribes that still bear the marks of their ancestor.

****

Why The Kiskadee Wears A Bandage On Its Head

During the time when the Earth was young and all creatures, whether Man or other animals, could have communicated one with the other, there lived on the Merume Plateau a large village of the People.

There was no enmity among The People. The first Carib had just arrived on Earth, but had not yet had any appreciable communion with the People. Animals, especially birds, harbored no ill-will among themselves and the predators since they fully understood the natural laws. Even the plants had just started evolving spines and spicules for the protection of themselves.
Once they could have seen that there was no fear among animals. But, they feared the dark. They feared things under water. They feared the Bush dai-dai and the Massacouroman, and the Moon-gazer. However they did not fear the Kanaima since he did not make his appearance among them. The People only feared the things that they could not explain nor understand. They still tried to explain them through the process of their natural environment.

They understood that sickness and disease were personalized and, hence, they had no fear of such. They endeavored not to offend the elements, and stringently avoided excesses. They took only what they needed and neither hoarded nor coveted.

154

But, this way of life was about to change. The woman Korobona, had jumped into the forbidden pool and touched a stump that had arisen above water. The stump had seized her and made her his wife. When she bore her first son, her brothers were jealous of the honors bestowed on their sister and wished to kill their nephew. They nonetheless changed their minds and spared him. The boy however soon died.

Korobona was very sad after this and returned to the forbidden pond and her husband. Soon she bore another son. It was from this son that the Carib descended to become a bane to the other tribes.

It was around this same time, too, that a handsome Arawak boy chose as his wife the beautiful daughter of King Vulture (Sarcoramphus papa). He married her in an elaborate ceremony and went, as was the custom, to live with his father-in-law. Because he was a very good husband and a provider, the Arawaks were always welcome among the Vultures. They always welcomed the excuse to throw elaborate cassiri parties whenever the Arawaks visited. This happened so many times at the bridegroom's expense that he felt a need for some reciprocity. He got extremely homesick and longed for some familiar surroundings.

One day he broached this need with his father-in-law. The elder became so enraged that he summoned all his robust male relatives. He related what the young man had told him embellishing it a little. They also became enraged, set upon the hapless young man and set him up the tallest Awara Palm tree (Astrocaryum tucumoides).

Not only was the awarra palm the tallest among the others but it was in the middle of a clump of others as well. Well, everyone knows of the terrible thorns of this ancient tree. It was the first plant to develop spines to prevent Monkey from climbing it up to drink the water from the young nuts. To other inhabitants, even the awara tree ought not to be destroyed for the fruit is at its best when ripe and not while still young.

The predicament in which the young Arawak Ihiki found himself seemed hopeless indeed. After the initial shock he thought of summoning his wife but, when he remembered that she was large with child, and how frail she was, he perished the thought. He even surmised that, even if she knew, she could be unable to help since she dared not disobey her father. There in the highest tree, Ihiki stayed for many moons. The sun burnt him during the day. The cold cramped his bones during the night and he was very miserable every time rain fell. However for all the physical pains he endured, his most uncomfortable moments came when he thought of his wife; so lithe and frail with her large limpid eyes as a scared doe in the forest. All the tender moments they ever shared passed through his mind as on a screen and made his misery doubly hard to endure. He was becoming weaker and weaker and resigned himself to die with his wife's image in his heart and her name on her lips. The last of a shower of rain roused him from his febrile reverie and slaked his parched throat so, when, he saw Brer Annancy and his wife searching for a safe and sheltered spot to incubate their eggs, Ihiki was hardly able to speak when Annancy enquired as to his predicament. He was lucky that he had got the little water to drink so he could make his voice audible.

When he had finished telling Annancy his story, he looked so lost and forlorn that Annancy took pity on him. Annancy and his wife huddled to one side and conferred for a while. Presently, the wife left and Annancy tried to cheer up Ihiki who was still in the throes of despondency.

When Mrs. Annancy returned, she returned with a retinue of relatives dogging her heels. All of them now started to spin a stout chord so that Ihiki could safely descend. When this task was satisfactorily accomplished, the weak Ihiki, supported by a host of his benefactors, was ceremoniously escorted back to the village.

The tribe was indeed glad to welcome Ihiki and his guests but was surprised at the state of his physical being. Ihiki's father thanked the Annancies and provided them with a big feast. After that, they left and Ihiki related his story to the Tribe. They were all sad, for they knew that they would never more be welcomed among the Vultures for they well knew that traditions were held sacred among all beings.

For many years Ihiki tried to get back to his wife. He failed because the Vultures would have nothing to do with him and foiled even his best-laid plans. However, at last, the other birds took compassion on his predicament and escorted him to the abode of the Vultures. The Vultures resented this and so the birds were forced to wage a fierce battle against the Vultures. This lasted for many days. The Vultures, against superior numbers, were forced to retreat to the innermost recesses of their home territories where only pee-zwing and bimiti could penetrate. The vultures easily repelled these miniscule creatures.

During the first half of the battle, however, Ihiki, on whose behalf the battle was waged, was slain by his own son, the son whom he never saw, and the son with whom he had become an outcast.

Now the birds retreated and formulated a new strategy to get at the Vultures. They decided to burn the home of the enemy.

They recalled all of the combatants, and recounted them. Something seemed to be wrong. Nowhere could they locate Kiskadee (Saurophagus sulfuratus). No one can remember to have seen him fallen in battle. Now, coming to think of it, no one could not even recall seeing him. They temporarily forgot this infraction as they carried out their plan and burned down the Vultures' homes.

When the fire was lit, some of the beautiful birds could be seen fleeing the inferno with the beautiful white crests on fire. Many were burnt coal black, and fell to the ground limping away in ignominy. This is why today the male of the vulture species carry a red head burnt that color by the birds on behalf of Ihiki. The females are all coal black, a legacy of their burnt dwellings and the defeat suffered at the hands of the other birds.

The spoils of war now had to be divided. One incident occurred that is worthy of mention. Trumpet bird and Heron could not agree over a trifle over which both claimed. So they fought and rolled each other in the now cold ashes. Trumpet bird, the weaker, was rolled all over by heron that was only thrown on his back by its weaker adversary. This caused trumpet bird to be grey all over while heron is only grey on its back.

When all was nearly finished, who should appear on the scene claiming his share although he had surreptitiously disdained to fight? He felt that he was equally entitled to a share of the spoils. Kiakadee, with a white bandage around his head emerged and demanded some of the goods.

He pretended to be ill and he spoke with vehemence when he was accused of being a coward. "I am as brave as any one of you. You all recall how I defended myself and my nest against horse-whip! If I had not got this terrible headache, I myself would have killed King Vulture without so much as batting an eye-lid".

All the birds saw through his ruse. His audience was convinced that he was not sincere about the so-called headache or his illness. They still deemed him a coward. From that day onward they compelled him to wear the bandage around his head for all times.

Kiskadee did not like this then since all saw through him. He does not like it now either. This is why he always attacks larger birds, whenever he can, to avenge the indignity he suffered so long ago.

(Above: the kiskadee – with white 'bandage' around his head. Source: <u>www.youtube.com</u>)

****

Why The Marudi Throat Is Red

(Above: the marudi, the national bird of Guyana. Source: www.ebay.ca)

Where the mists of the morning dew meet the undulating surface of the "Gran Sabana," there lies, about sixty-six miles from the apex of the Roraima Formation, the village of Uacauyen. Its location just above the confluence of the Caroni with the Aponquao and this makes this village ideally suited for the defense against the Hooronis that descend periodically from the recesses of the sandstone plateau to raid the villages of the lowland.

The Caroni is a great branch of the mighty Orinoco and, as such, has great religious significance to the people when decisions regarding their welfare had to be made. So, when Makonaima decreed that the Descendants of the People settle at this particular confluence, there was hardly ever any dissension, since Chief Manihot explained that it was the Great One himself that has decreed that this location was the most ideal.

The reason was that, since Makonaima's abode was in the north-western side of Roraima and the sun strikes exactly at an acute angle at seven o'clock on a certain date, then, where the end of the shadow falls on this propitious day, must be located the Village of the Flame.

You see, since Makonaima has chosen to locate his abode on the rain-ward side of the escarpment, fire was very hard to keep for any extended period of time. So, he decreed that, whenever the shadow of the sun falls on the low land on this particular date, there would arise a village that would be the perpetual keeper of the flames. So, the village of Ucauyen arose in the exact spot where the shadow of the top of Roraima Mountain touches the lowland at 7 a. m. of the vernal equinox. This is the westernmost limit of the shadow at this hour. Before, the entire area is encompassed in an aura of surreal light only seen in this single spot in the entire world.

From this hour of seven, as if by magic, the whole area is bathed in brilliant sunlight, be it rainfall or fog, and heats up with a gradual luminescence and intensity that belies old Sol's mercilessness in these regions. At this village of Uacauyen, Chief Manihot was entrusted with the keeping of the flame for always. During this time also the Southern Cross lived on the Grand Sabana and the dew on the grass was still the spittle of the stars. The Southern Cross visited the village of Uacauyen and even took "Counta" faggot and gave Chief Manihot advice on the sustenance of the fire. The size of the flame was not important once the embers were hot. The wood "Counta" was known to keep a flame whether the wood was green, wet, dry or dank. So, once the initial fire is lit, this is the most ideal wood to use.

All this happened just after the Great Flood when Makonaima descended from his lofty abode.

Man was now instructed to make fire and how to keep it for the use of Makonaima's people.

The houses of the village had now been constructed and the animals descended from their lofty abode to live among men from their erstwhile cramped quarters on the Great Ite. Makonaima now gave his advice to the Chief and disappeared to his lofty abode to listen to the supplications of his people.

Chief Manihot now placed the mortar-piece between his two insteps and the pestle in the shallow hole with shredded mahoe (hibiscus tillicus) bark and rapidly started to spin the pestle piece between the palms of his hands. All the animals were lolling around, some cogitating on their future while some were still trying to get out the cricks from their joints. But, curious Marudi positioned himself to the right of the Chief, close to the angle of his bent thigh and calf.

Now everyone can attest to the curiosity of the Marudi. Marudi loves shiny things and is very fond of insects and will pursue and catch them even on the wings. So, as Marudi crouched by the leg of Chief Manihot, he was so intent on the fire making activity that he seemed entranced, so closely focused was he.

Suddenly, a tiny curl of smoke snaked sideways and then upward. Marudi sat tense and spellbound. Presently a red glow appeared among the tinder as a first spark. Chief Manitou was perspiring profusely. As a huge bead of perspiration rolled down into his right eye, he temporarily closed it. As he did so, his right hand went up involuntarily to ease his discomfort. At this opportune moment Marudi's neck darted out with wide, opened beak and swallowed the spark mistaking it for a firefly, and then flew quickly away.

The initial spark, considered holy, burned the Marudi's throat. This is the reason why, to this day, Marudi carries a red wattle on his throat.

In the meanwhile, poor alligator (caiman in fact), that was very close, opened his gaping mouth to yawn as he closed his eyes and let out a bored grunt. As the Chief took his hand from his eyes, he realized that the spark that he had worked so very hard was stolen. Observing the alligator with his open mouth, who was, during this time, quite a gentle creature, albeit ugly, lazing nearby, the chief readily suspected him of stealing the spark.

When the Chief made known his suspicion, the other animals readily agreed with him. So, without any evidence, save their abhorrence and dislike for the ugliness of the alligator, they all beset on him with their fists, claws and wings and tore poor alligator's tongue out in their search for the spark. Alligator was not even given a chance to protest, defend or protect himself. This is the very reason why, all the descendants of alligator have only a rudimentary tongue up to this day, while Marudi carries the red throat as a mark of the theft that he carried out so long ago.

There is one fall-out from this. Since that day onwards alligator continues to carry a grudge against all animals.

****

TRAVELS and SETTLEMENTS - NAMES

The Settlement Of Issano

They emerged out of the mists of the Peamah Falls in the upper Mazuruni just after the big rains.

They have been travelling for almost a month now. The People left their homeland at Lchabaru in Venezuela because their hunting grounds have been gradually taken over by foreigners with red beards who had superior weaponry. Of course, the land was not then known as Venezuela, but as Cumanacaibo, and the people was known simply as the "People".

The People said that they were the descendants of the Sky People who came to earth eons ago. These people had a peaceful life, having many strange adventures in the land they had come to love as their home.

Their main activity was hunting for the aguti and paca, but most of all, they loved to hunt the giant water rat that dwelt on the forest fringe of the great llanos.

These animals were so numerous that they formed the main source of protein for the People who caught and ate so many so that it was not strange in visiting the benab of any one of the scattered families to be entertained with this succulent flesh cooked in liberal amounts of casreep and chili peppers.

On leaving any of the forested household, it was customary to load up the stranger with vittles good for many days' journey. This was not done because the stranger might starve during his wanderings, but it was the custom practiced by generations of The People, as long as anyone could remember.

It must be noted that any stranger was quite capable of foraging for himself; but this was just the custom. The environment was well blessed and little effort was needed to obtain sustenance.

The People spent some time below the falls fashioning wood-skin corials from the huge purple-heart trees found in this region. At the same time they caught huge amounts of pacu and haimara, which they dried and stored in their makeshift benabs.

The weather was much cooler in this region than the one they had left and, thus the people never did entertain the idea of settling permanently in the area. Except the cold, never a day seemed to pass without excessive downpours, which made every article feel damp for the greater part of the time. They always had to keep their dried fish over the fire in case it should spoil.

The two leaders, Pia and his elder brother, Makonaima, held a council and they all decided that they must move farther down river in search of a more suitable place to develop a permanent settlement.

As they travelled slowly down river, despite the strong currents, they made many periodic stops and foraged along the banks, sometimes spending many days in one location. Many miles down-river, they gathered parapi, turu and other edible nuts and fruits. At Kamakusa they found a huge sawari tree loaded with nuts. This place looked quite enchanting since there was fish in abundance also, while the forests teemed with powis, maam, marudi and duraquqrra.

The climate was not so cold but the ground was stony and shallow. Although their minds were not fully made up, they decided to tarry a while. So, they cleared some land and planted cassava and yams, sugar cane, tomato and melons. The yield was hardly adequate but this stop served to protect their planting materials for another season.

The stay at Kamakusa was not altogether unhappy, but there seemed to be some basic component that was missing. Although there was no shortage of food or shelter, the easy smile and spontaneous laughter seemed to be absent. The Chiefs seemed to have noticed this; so, one night they called all the people to the communal area. They decided that the only fault that they have found was with the shallow land but they would not leave the area until they have reaped their produce and save as much planting materials as possible to start some new cultivation in a more suitable location.

After some time, when all was ready, the Chiefs gave the order to load the wood skins. The morning was cool and clear with just a hint of fog on the surface of the water. The day, as all knew, will be dazzling bright and the weather would be fine.

They travelled in relative ease for two days, occasionally landing and exploring the environment at the side of the river when the sound ahead proclaimed the waters to be dangerous. It was now getting to be near the end of the dry season and the water in the river was indeed low. This made the "shooting" of rapids with craft such as theirs extremely dangerous. The Chiefs sent out a small wood-skin ahead to seek out a way. Orders were given to hug the near bank to land and scout a passage down the rapids, which they subsequently dubbed, "Tiboko", when they had subsequently made it down to the foot of the rapids.

After about three hours the scout craft returned to report that "running" the rapids with crafts such as they had was impossible. The series of falls stretched entirely across the river and so it was impossible to use the river as a way forward.

In the background, from the inner sanctum of the forest, could be heard the unending sound of the bell-bird regularly sending forth "tin-tin-abulation" to penetrate with slow deliberation the slow echoing b-o-n-g as it travels with seemingly unending penetration, slowly producing a silent echo, which seemed to slowly die in the vastness of the forest.

In contrast to the doleful and slowly piercing note could also be heard the sound of the "pi-pi-yo", which cried its name through the day with this beautiful sound echoing sharply through the forest. In the foreground, newborn cicadas could be heard as hardly discernible background music as they vibrated their wings even as their backs split, having just passed on their genes in one of the opposite sex.

Having portaged their worldly goods overland to the foot of the falls and safely eased their wood-skins and canoes down to the bottom of the falls, they reloaded and paddled downstream to meet the Paradise described above.

Maybe the gradual recuperation from their efforts, the seemingly harmony and solemnity of the entire area encouraged the decision that they have met their Eden. They decided that they had finally arrived at the ideal place that they started searching for so many moons ago. The brothers, after examining the surroundings, finally decided to make this place their permanent settlement.

Having satisfied their hunger, the older males left to explore the vicinity while the younger sought suitable places to locate their camps.

Presently, Makonaima and his entourage returned to report the most beautiful country of gently sloping hills and valleys, with the most deep and fertile land suitable for farming. And, best of all, the giant Merume Mountains formed a fitting background to the landscape. They also found numerous traces of tapir and peccary, deer, and numerous wild birds.

Around the campfire that night everyone agreed that this idyllic and untouched Eden was the ideal spot for them to set up their permanent habitation.

Each family selected their own sites and soon houses were erected for every family while a huge communal field was cleared and planted. During all this time the men made regular forages into the surrounding areas where they soon returned with more than adequate game for the pot. The main river and its tributaries also provided huge amounts of fish. They only had to leave a few fish traps or a few "spring-hooks" to collect an adequate amount of fish in the morning.

One very "religious" experience occurred one morning at about dawn when Pia and Makonaima went out to retrieve fish from their traps. They had just turned a bend some distance upriver when, as they looked up, there seemed to be a flash of lightning. Suddenly in the distance, the entire Merume escarpment lit up. The river seemed jet-black in contrast to the brightly illuminated sandstone face of the mountains. The brothers were gazing from darkest light to brilliant daylight and, as the golden rays of the sun traversed the vertical face of the mountains, gleaming silicates seemed to reflect all the myriad colors of Creation as the sun slowly and silently changed as it ascended over the dark tops of the verdant forest.

Whilst this was unfolding, the faces of long dead ancestors seemed as if temporarily etched, albeit fleetingly, in the light and shade of the sandstone facade. The brothers remained still as this wondrous spectacle unfolded and remained so until it passed. It was the most beautiful scenery ever witnessed by the brothers. They were so dazzled and in awe that they completely forgot their mission. It was long after this wondrous spectacle unfolded and faded into oblivion that they remembered their fish-traps.

The next morning the entire village made a pilgrimage to this particular part of the river from where this wondrous sight was witnessed. They went early. With bated breath, each waited to witness this soul full-filling spectacle. As the sun rose and lit up the escarpment they beheld a scene, which they agreed was a shrine of their ancestors. Each of the older seemed to recognize a loved one long past. The phenomenon faded and they returned to their newly found village in the belief that this was indeed their "Promised Land."

After their second Mashramani feast, when the field had been cleared and planted Makonaima was visited by a strange dream. He was instructed by the Great Spirit to cross the watershed and enter the great Essequibo. From there he was instructed to journey for many days until he reached the great tributary on his right. His instruction further said that he must climb the tableland from which the Father of the Waters issued and there to settle with his family.

He left the village, which he and his brother had founded and did as he was instructed and, suffice it to say, we have heard tales of his great deeds in quelling the war among the tribes and, ultimately, of his ultimate sacrifice to the God of Waters.

Pia ruled over the people of Issano wisely and long, and his village formed a great stopover for the many tribes trading between the mouth of the Orinoco and the Guiana Savannahs. His tribe prospered and their settlement can still be found inland from the southern end of the Bartica-Issano road.

Anyone who wants to experience the spiritual upliftment first felt by Pia and Makonaima only has to station himself on the ever-placid waters in the dark of the fore-dawn "top-side" of Issano and watch as Sol lights up Merume escarpment in regal majesty.

(Above: aerial view of Issano Settlement, Guyana. Source: www.en.wikipedia.org)

The Legend Of Ituribisci

The Legend of Ituribisci is little known by outsiders. But the lake of that name and the creek that issues from its tranquil waters were once classified as a tourist attraction and frequently visited by locals and foreigners alike. This happened to be the case because of the phenomenon of having cold water in one side of the lake while the other side had water the temperature of which could readily allowed brewing of tea.

There was a continuous flow of water on the surface and, if one had the time and the inclination to, then that person can easily position his water craft, being canoe of batteau, in such a position as to have cold water on one side and very warm water on the other side of the craft.

Although this lake was well known by the people on the Arabian Coast, only some actually visited it since domestic activities demanded most of their waking hours and most of their time. Acquiring the necessities of life took up most of their waking hours and left little time for leisure time activities. Visiting this interesting location was mostly the pursuit of Outsiders who can afford leisure time activities.

The position, quality and other attributes of the phenomenon were known by all local people as intimately as if everyone had visited it although not one of them had ever been.

The people who regularly visited, stayed, or passed, were the Amerindians. Long before the Missionaries established a Mission there, the Amerindians from Bethany Mission on the Arahuria Creek on a branch of the Supenaam had known the area and constantly used the route passing through the "Three Sisters" area, and not only to stop and worship, but overnight also on their way to the Pomeroon. Somehow or the other, the locals regarded the area as a hallowed area which caused the subsequent building of a Mission House there. Not only the Natives but, nearly everyone who knew the area, came to regard the area as the holiest place of pilgrimage and worship on the Essequibo. At one time there was a visiting priest that conducted Services every Sunday.

Long before the Dutch and other European nations penetrated the area, it formed a stopover on the trade route that supplied both the Orinoco delta and the Savannahs with trade goods that were so essential to comfortable existence. There were found Wai-wai hunting dogs throughout the entire route of the northeastern coast. Wild rice from the Orinoco delta was planted in the Rupununi savannahs. The huge yellow silver balli and cedar canoes were valuable items of trade. The long powerful bows made from the exotic letter-wood tree were found throughout the entire area, as were turtle shell trinkets and other articles of not only utilitarian but also artistic value.

There never was a permanent settlement of many houses in the Lake Ituribisci, (maybe until lately). Maybe the mere nature of its sanctity and the silent sable waters, the gentle breezes that reversed their directions between morning and afternoon, seemed to lend a sort of majesty and mystery to the place and add to the tranquil holiness of the environment.

The Amerindians respected the inexplicable and wondrous nature of the environment and, thus, camped only as long as was necessary to rest themselves on their journey among villages on the mission of trade.

It happened so many moons ago when Makonaima left Pia to settle on the bank of the Mazaruni at Issano. He himself crossed the Essequibo watershed, went up the Potaro and settled on the Kaieteur Plateau. Both groups of people prospered greatly and soon production outstripped demand. Men of the tribe now had ample time to explore and travel, and indulge in other pursuits and specialize in various occupations. While the people of Makonaima were known far and wide for their blow guns, the people of Issano were known for their very light and versatile silverballi canoe. So light was it that four young men can lift one and portage it a very long distance over rough terrain if needs be.

Despite their subsistence life style, small groups periodically set out to explore the resources of their environment. As they became more familiar with their surroundings, they went further and further afield after every expedition. Makonaima's People headed in a northeast direction until they reached the great Cuyuni River. They caught the varied variety of fishes that teemed at the foot of the cataracts and waterfalls that adorned this river, the bosom of which great ribbon of water was slightly rough. They shot and snared some of the abundant game that inhabited the banks of this fruitful river. The travelers could easily obtain an abundance of food to preserve for further exploration. While some stayed in the areas to consolidate their positions, others returned home to report of their prosperity.

After some time and more visits, it was decided that larger parties explore and establish base camps and so to extend further and further.

By this time Pia's group had already crossed the great river nearer its mouth, followed a narrow branch stream to its headwaters, and launched their light crafts on the northeastern flowing Supenaam. This river started its flow on the northeastern side of the Blue Mountains, which form the watershed. After about eighty tortuous miles this river empties its water near the mouth of the giant Essequibo River. When these easterly travelers encountered muddy waters in the Supenaam, they decided to go no further, travelled up a tributary where no muddy water goes and established their settlement on a very beautiful hill. (This idyllic place will become a permanent settlement, which exists up to today and is known as the famous Arahuria Mission) Today it even boasts an airstrip.

Having settled in this fertile spot, they explored further and further until they reached a wet savannah. They could now leave the creek and paddle in any direction they wished. This area was dotted with clumps of white cedar and moco-moco and other nondescript and unfamiliar greenery while, along the creeks, the majestic ite palms grew in regal splendor in all stages of height. As the travelers glided among these giants they wondered at the difference in the landscape of the mountains and felt liberated in this open expanse.

Ahead on the left the savannah seemed an ever-open expanse, while on the right a low range of hills beckoned the travelers with its blue green haze.

The travelers followed the creek and headed into an opening between the two hills which stream appear to end in a small waterfall. The cool waters seemed to beckon the travelers after the heat of the open savannahs. They refreshed themselves from their store and climbed the slope to explore. They soon started to descend on the other side of the hill since the saddle seemed to form a sort of watershed. They returned, portaged their canoe and were soon in a stream that led into a large tranquil lake.

Presently Marika put his hand down to slake his thirst and nearly yelled. The expression on his face brought a silent query from his companions. Marika pointed to the water and beckoned them to try. They were shocked to feel the temperature of the water; it was so cold as to cause goose bumps to appear on the arms and torsos of some of the paddlers.

They beached their canoe and made an early camp. They were so surprised that no one took a regular bath that night. The superstitious even thought that the water would not get hot to cook that evening. However, the water behaved as usual, and this seemed somewhat to allay the superstition that was threatening their primeval minds.

Meanwhile, Makonaima's people, crossed the Cuyuni many miles upstream from Pia's group. They skirted the Blue mountain on the western side and, the day before Marika and his crew left Toparo and his men, navigated an easterly flowing stream, and paddled out on the bosom of the lake on the exact other side from which Marika and his men were encamped.

Great was their surprise when they discovered the water so warm that they surmised that Manitou was good to them and had rewarded them for the cold time they were spending on the Kaieteur Plateau, albeit their fantastic prosperity. They bathed and frolicked and made their camp a little way from the sandy beach. The next day, they went in to explore the surrounding forests and, although they encountered game, they did not attempt to kill any. They did not fail to experience and notice the sanctity and the holy tranquility of the place.

They left their camp the next morning in silence and awe and retraced their steps. After a speedy and uneventful journey, they reached their camp on the other side of the Cayuni. They instantly related their adventure to their companions who listened in disbelief as the lips of Toparu revealed the highlight of their journey. What, however, enthralled the more mature listeners was the description of the serenity and sanctity of their discovery!

After settling in, Marika and his men related a very different adventure from the one told by Toparu and his men. He claimed that the water was so hot that it was capable of softening the turu with which they made a nourishing and delicious drink. In fact they had just done that for two days.

"That's impossible," shouted the more fiery Marika. "That lake was so cold that, when I went out one mid-day for a dip my teeth chattered so loudly that my men laughed at me."

"Are you sure of the direction that you took and that both of us discovered the same lake?" asked Toparu. "Let's go in the yard and draw in the sand the routes that we both took."

This was agreed to and both the leaders took their men and went in the sandy yard and delineated the routes that they took.

After smoothing the sand, they both agreed that an X marked their present location. Then each drew the streams and hills and other landmarks that they encountered and crossed along with the amount of time spent at each location. They detailed all their activities from leaving to returning. No sooner had they finished that they realized that their erstwhile destinations were about two miles from each other before the return journey was effected.

Several times they repeated their journeys in the sand and every time each claimed that he could not be mistaken. Each was now convinced that they were talking about the same body of water. There could be no mistake. Tension seemed to divide the villages as each person took one side or the other.

The idea of visiting the same lake and at different places seemed to be the only logical conclusion from the drawings and discussions.

Marika, having arrived first and left early, seemed to recall that on their last evening, the scent of the "Haiawa", (a sweet smelling resinous crystal obtained by bleeding the hiawa tree and burnt as an incense), startled him and made him suspect that they were not alone. This memory caused Marika to waver in his conviction and soften his attitude. He was, however, unconvinced that it was the identical lake that each had visited.

Tensions grew among the populace and the two Chiefs were

summoned. Runners left and, within one week, the two chiefs were ensconced on the dais of honor prepared for them. Both Toparu and Marika were made to redraw their crude maps and relate their stories for the benefit of all. Forthwith, it was decided that Toparu and Marika, their peimen and paddlers would retrace Toparu's route.

Early the next morning the men set out in four canoes. Very soon (two days after) they were over the saddle and into the lake. No sooner than they were on the placid surface of the lake that, Toparu, having recognized the former landing site, ordered the men to stop paddling. With the greatest poise and gravity he bade the Chiefs to dip their hands into the tranquil waters.

They gravely confirmed that Toparu was correct. The rest of the men lost no time in confirming the matter. Even Marika seemed to confirm that this seemed to be the same lake that he and his men visited not so long ago. The sun, he noticed, was in a different direction. So, if this was the same lake, he obviously entered it from the opposite direction.

Far off on the opposite shore the background of the shore seemed to look familiar. Whilst he was just cogitating this, he blurted out, "Let's all paddle to the far shore," pointing to the opposite bank.
They all agreed and soon the crews of the four canoes dipped the thin blades of their paddles in the cool dark water and went in the direction indicated.

They soon reached the middle of the lake and, without thinking, Pia dipped his hand in the water. He was surprised that it had lost its frigid temperature. He however kept it to himself. Marika presently recognized a landmark on the shoreline and then was convinced that here was where he had entered the lake on the previous visit. He directed the men to make their way to a certain spot. He recognized that this end was much shallower and the water exhibited a more sparkling and lighter color. He soon recognized the small inlet where they had entered the lake. On arriving at this placid bay he bade the Chief and uncle to immerse their hands in the water. Great was their surprise when they discovered that the water was very warm indeed. Marika now asked the Chiefs on land so he could show them evidence of their previous visit and so convinced one and all that he was also right, though none doubted him in the least now.

All went a little inland since they decided to spend their time on this shore. Some powis tails were erected and they spent the night comfortably.

The next morning, at the direction of the peimen, a spot was selected to erect a shrine to the Great One who so subtly provided such a contrast in the same body of water.

After a Council was held, it was decided that, since Manitou was so kind as to lead his children to so wondrous a spot, the area, and especially the lake, would remain a holy place to the People, not to live, but as a shrine and continuous reminder of the goodness and greatness of Manitou.

It remained thus, only a place of worship of the tribes who now constantly pass through on their travels to trade, or just fraternize. It was known far and wide among the tribes as a gift of the Great One and a shrine where wishes were made and granted. Some even claimed to be healed after prayers and a bath in these contrasting waters were offered for them in this area. Miraculous happenings were also attributed not only to the lake but also the entire area.

As the white Men penetrated the area in the post Colombian times, they heard of this fabulous lake. Their Missionaries even built a Church on the spot of the original shrine. When they Christianized the natives, these People still make the Mission a special place of worship; maybe not so much to worship the new Deity, but also to commune with the sanctity of the place and the old Spirits.

Today the lake is still there although the Mission is a mere memory. However, the old memory lives on and the holiness is still experienced by those who have not yet succumbed themselves to the artificiality of modern civilization. In the late evening, or early morning, depending on which side of the lake you are, the uninitiated might still experience the holiness of the place once he lets himself be steeped in its tranquility.

Of late, however, it is learned that, because of the so-called development encroachments on the shores of the lake and the adjoining forests, the contrasting temperatures are slowly being equalized. Whether it is a price to pay for development or it is the curse of Manitou; it may never be known. Losing this phenomenon is the loss of a National Spiritual Legacy. This is sad.

May the legend of Ituribisci live on in the minds of all those who care to cherish the "Legends of the First Peoples".

(Above: Lake Ituribisci, Essequibo County, Guyana. Source: www.caribbeanbeat.com)

****

The Capoey Story

An old friend, who lived all his life as a Native of the Essequibo Coast, Guyana South America, told this story to me. As long as he could remember, he said, he lived a life of ease on the sandy rim of Lake Capoey, about six miles inland from the Atlantic Ocean on the Essequibo Coast.

With a penchant for detail and the memory of a Griot, Matthew took two nights and copious draughts of warrup and bilteri to narrate what I am now about to write.

One further word before I begin. For those who care to remember, the whole of the Essequibo Coast was once known as Capoey. The history books will tell you that, when the slaves left the sugar estates after Emancipation, they migrated to the urban areas. After indentureship when a Berbice or a Demerara relative was to visit anyone on the Essequibo Coast and was asked where he/she was going, he/she would invaribly reply, "Capoey". How the entire Arabian Coast became to be called Capoey may be lost to antiquity, or might be a matter for conjecture. But, for people of Matthew's caliber who keep stories alive by oft-times repeating them to the generations that come after them, it will always be real.

According to Matthew: As the sun was approaching the western horizon across the narrow strip of water that forms the Dragon's Mouth between the Mainland and Trinidad, where the village of Chaguna was located on the tip of the Northern Range, sub-chief Rana, of the branch of Caribs who inhabited this idyllic area, had his mind far away. His mental environment was a complete contrast to his physical one. As he gazed across the waters with a distant and melancholy look in his eyes, the fascination of dusk across the strait (which never failed to awe him) was lost this afternoon in his present somber mood.

His encounter with Juan Martinez the week before would have remained his secret alone if he had followed his instinct and scuttled the sick stranger's canoe in the Gulf. Probably because of the emaciated and half-starved mien, the languorous look on the bony visage, or the wan look of the individual, Rana took pity on this hapless individual. Rana solemnly and slowly took his water gourd and put it to the lips of Martinez.

As soon as some of the water trickled down the side of his mouth and few drops entered between his discolored teeth, this served to revive hm. As he opened his eyes, he seemed so helpless, piteous and harmless that Rana's heart seemed to open up in empathy. Rana pulled in his fish line, tied the stranger's canoe alongside his, and paddled both ashore.

On shore Rana readily installed the visitor into his hut. Discussion with the stranger continued far into the night. At last it was decided by the Chief, in consultation with his Elders, that the stranger be escorted east and delivered to the governor De Berrio. This was done the next day. The rescuers were thanked and dispatched with ample gifts to return to their village.

Slowly afterwards, rumors started to reach Chaguna of a fantastic tale told to the Spaniards by Martinez.

An emissary had already been sent to interview sub-chief Rana with regard to what and what was told to him by Martinez when he was rescued. None of the Natives believed such tales as told to them by Martinez when he was rescued, and dismissed his rantings as a ploy to be accorded good treatment, or to De Berrios method, to have another discussion to hear what Martinez divulged, was interpreted by the leaders of the village as a new ploy to get new recruits to work on their newly opened Missions and mines that they had established both on the Venezuelan mainland and the island. So, on this second tete-a-tete they sent only old men. This method had been employed before with a forceful transportation of a dozen young and able-bodied men not so long ago. These young men were never seen nor heard from again.

Immediately the Emissary left, the Chief called his Council for a discussion. The decision taken was that, to abort any raid on their village when De Berrio had seen that they had seen through his ploy, was that the entire village would be divided into two parties and immediately escape to the mainland far from their village. The Chief and party will travel west when they crossed to the mainland, while Rana and the other set will travel towards and beyond the Orinoco delta. This will serve to confuse any likely pursuers since they will not know which set to follow.

As soon as the curtain of night descended as reluctantly across the Gulf and Strait, sub-chief Rana's mind was in great turmoil. This was not only because of the unknown dangers that might lie ahead, but also he felt like a traitor about the abandonment of his beloved Cayuga, which he dearly loved. And on the other hand, the abandonment of so many other friends from the adjoining villages who he will never see again, though some of them were related consanguinally.

Sub-chief Ran gazed one last time and saw the faint sliver of a crescent moon accompanying the darkening sun as it sank behind the primeval forest of the mainland. This opined sub-chief Rana to himself is an omen that portrays a loss of both tribe and family. However, the decision had been taken and must be carried out in its entirety. As soon as darkness descended on the landscape, the entire village loaded all their belongings into four large canoes and, with fond farewells, left each other in the middle of the Strait to pursue their separate paths. Two canoes pointed their bows westwards while the other two, with Rana and his entourage, started skirting the shore in the direction of the Orinoco delta.

Although Rana and his followers explored many of the distributaries of this great river, they deemed none with suitable land for a permanent settlement. They have been accustomed to well-drained and sloping land with wooded hills and valleys. The delta was swampy and humid and mosquito-ridden. They soon encountered the natives of the Mainland, the Warraus. The life they lived was so different as to seem primitive by Carib standards. What, however spurred Rana and his group ever onwards on their quest for a better land, was the rumors that the Spaniards had Missions on some of the rivers.

Like in Trinidad, the Spaniards recruited the natives to work on the Missions as virtual slaves. They therefore bypassed all the Spanish Settlements. After Muraco, they gave the Islas de Pajoras a wide berth. They later encountered a large vessel out at sea paddled by some natives. They claimed that they were from the Mission San Frisco de Guayo. This reinforced the belief of sub-chief Rana and his men of the fact that slavery was not very far away.

Three days after encountering the vessel from the Mission, they entered a river that ran in another direction to that of the Orinoco and its distributaries. The sub-chief surmised that this could not be the Orinoco since it ran in a southeasterly direction. He recalled that, when he had found Martinez so emaciated in the Gulf and learned that he was at the mercy of the wind and currents for many days, he might have exited from any one of the distributaries of the Orinoco; or, more likely, was pushed by the Coastal current that entered the Gulf through the Serpent's mouth from a river as the one he now was entering.

The aim of Rana's quest was not for what the Spaniards valued but to put himself as far away from slavery as he could. This direction, he took into the new river was co-incident with the direction which he envisaged will take him furthest from any likely pursuers who may want to validate Martinez's story with that which the Spaniards felt that Martinez had told to Rana and made him speed swifter onwards. He felt that he could not trust any Spaniards at the rate with which news could have been spread.

Once in the Waini, far from the Great Salt Waters, a sense of tranquility seemed to have enveloped the entire group and imbued the wayfarers with a sense of security. They now landed to replenish their store of food from the nearby forests. This done, they felt at ease as they paddled up the Waini without thinking in the least about time nor distance.

One day they encountered a band of hunters who were obviously of Arawak origin. These hunters were setting fish traps to catch the schools of morocot that were travelling upriver to spawn. They learnt that the morocot-trappers were part of a much bigger band that was on the coast.

Being of a very suspicious nature, the strangers threw out hints about the red-bearded strangers, about the surrounding country, and about the Warraus who they left behind and also about any strangers and their customs. Understandably, the strangers were hesitant to divulge the exact location of their main body until they could ascertain with certainty that the strangers were above board.

Before they had left the islands, a long time ago, they were aware of the ferocity of the Caribs. However, to have encountered them in such a humble position, they readily assured the strangers of one fact that there were no Spanish settlements, mines or Missions for many days journey either by land or by canoe.

The strangers spent three days assisting in catching, gutting and drying the morocot. They soon also gathered enough for themselves since the fish seemed to be perpetually journeying upstream in such numbers as to defy the imagination. The traps were quickly set, emptied and reset. All the men were engaged in dressing the bounty. They also had enough for themselves as they toiled in the mosquito-less atmosphere, these pests being effectively kept at bay by the copious amounts of smoke, which not only made the area tolerable but also filled the atmosphere with the heady aroma of roasting protein.

During the stay with these fishers they were encouraged by them to travel across the country to see the main body, whom they learnt were also gathering food on the Coastal Region. After a half a day across a tongue of land they encountered the entire tribe who was comfortably accommodated in comfortable camps. They had gathered huge amounts of turtle meat and smoked the delicacy and also had huge baskets of smoked turtle eggs slowly dehydrating over a slow fire. The main group was joined later in the day by a smaller group who brought many quakes (baskets) of living blue-backed crabs, some of them with huge claws. These crabs were caught some distance away in a salt marsh.

What impressed sub-chief Rana and his group was the ease with which huge amounts of food were obtained. Why did the tribes not choose the area as the ideal one to live? The Arawak leader explained that they used to live in the area once, but Spaniards who were passing in their ships readily spotted the smoke from their settlement. The Spaniards made periodic raids on the settlements and so they were forced to abandon any coastal areas. They would not now spend long on the coast but will quickly gather and retreat south and inland from the coastal areas.

There are no Spanish settlements south or west of here the Chief assured sub-chief Rana. Since it was now a week since the party came into the area, the main body packed and left early in the evening. One dozen sturdy men were left to assist the strangers while they made their preparations for departure. The men helped to portage the canoes over the neck of land. After this was done the entire group made their way, also under the cover of darkness, to the village of their hosts of the South.

Rana and his people enjoyed the hospitality of the Arawak People for some time. Although the surroundings teemed with life, the environ was mostly swampy. The Caribs longed for long sloping sandy beaches and land that was easily cultivable. This they intimated to the Chief. So, after many sessions of discussion, the travelers decided that they would travel farther south to settle. So, when the Arawaks left the next time for their land of turtle and fish, the visitors packed and moved south.

The Arawak Chief had hinted about a few lakes and elevated land some days march along the trade route in the direction of the interior. It is this trail that the strangers embarked on in their search for a suitable place to settle. As the hosts departed to their foraging grounds the Caribs pushed their canoes into the swampy savannahs. They followed a trail indistinguishable to the untrained eye until, after three days and nights, when they landed at the sandy edge of a hill where a feint trail seemed to lead into the forest, which was probably made by the aforementioned traders.

As soon they landed, their trained eyes detected three beached canoes slightly hidden in some thick bushes a little way from the trail. This discovery assured them that they were on some sort of trail used by travelers, probably the traders they heard mentioned of in the village of the Arawaks. They unloaded and did the same with their canoes taking care to hide them on the opposite side from which they found the others, taking care to sink them and cover them in the event they might need to use them in the future.

They were astonished for, as soon as they left the shoreline of the savannah, the trail became wider and more discernible but seemed only to be used occasionally. This, they agreed, must be the trade route between the tribes. They took an instant liking for the area and, once having travelled some distance inland, they made camp and explored the surroundings. Some was for settling right there but the majority was for moving on. This they did until they came to the edge of a most beautiful lake. They were elated. They readily pitched their camps and settled in. They lived happily in this area for some time and planted crops and fished and hunted and had the most comfortable life imaginable.

One day, as three young men were hunting, they met another group. Cautiously the groups made approaches one with the other and within the hour the three men agreed to accompany the others to their village.

After some discussion with the new group it was discovered that only one day's journey away was another more beautiful lake. When they returned to their own village some young men then joined their Chief Rana back on a journey to see the new settlement to which they have been invited. They were readily surprised at the serenity and peaceful atmosphere of this area. The soil seemed to be more fertile than the place where Rana's people lived.

As the young men were entertained in the guest hut, they were surprised to be served by bevies of beautiful maidens. Having been so long on the trail, for more than a year, this scene of domesticity seemed to appeal very strongly to their sensibilities.

Rana discovered that, in the endless migrations of people, they might develop peculiar cultural idiosyncrasies. These people he discerned to be different from both the Warraus and the Arawaks. After nights of story-telling by elders of the settled tribe, Rana and his entourage discovered that they were really kin to these people. The Warrau and the Arawaks were from very different bloodlines and cultural upbringing from the tribe, which said that that they are the true Caribs. He found out that, although they call themselves Ackawaios, they belonged to a branch of true Caribs as he himself is. During their storytelling they recalled their migrations from the islands of the Caribbean eons ago before the Spaniards were on the scene. They even discovered linguistic features between their languages. For example, both people call the sun "weya", or "weyana", potable water "toonah", arrow "porou", or "puro".

As communication between these two people grew, the overabundance of sons in the tribe of Rana naturally sought wives from among the people who were living on the shore of the smaller lake.

The first marriage took place between the son of Chief Rana whose name was "Apo', or " fire" and the daughter of a very respected elder. The girl's name was Onishena, which means "the rain" or "water". This name was given to her since she was born during one excessive rainy season. She was a tall, slender and beautiful girl. Her friends call her "Hairena" or "beautiful as the wild plantain." She was a fitting wife for Apo and all agreed that the match was most suitable.

It was a custom that both the bride and groom must agree on one thing that they will name together before they were made to flex and elongate the matapi as a sign of marriage. After this the name of the object beast or place will forever bear the name assigned to it by the married couple.

Since it was such a momentous occasion, both of the betrothed decided to rename the area in which they would live. Since it was customary that the groom goes to live at the bride's village, then they would have to rename her village.

One evening as the lovers stood at the sandy edge of the lake gazing into the placid waters, the moon rose above the trees and its reflection appeared in brilliant splendor in the water as it hung in regal splendor out of a cloudless sky. Apo held the hand of his Hairena and gazed at the reflection in the lake and silently uttered,"Noonah", the Carib name for moon,

"Kapoo-i," intoned Onishena.

"Noonah", said Apo.

"Kapoo-i", countered Onishena.

Apo gazed in the limpid eyes of his lover, took a deep breath and slowly agreed,"Kapoo-i." And that is how the lake and the village came to be called Capoey.

Matthew took a long draft of his warrup. "What do you think of my story?" he queried.

(Above: settlement at Lake Capoey. Source: www.guyanachronicle.com)

****

Im Thurn's Failure

It was just after Im Thurn and his band of explorers arrived at Arewa that the peace of the area seemed to be broken and there developed a kind of inexplicable tension. After the guests were accommodated in suitable lodgings and having become completely relaxed, it was the wish of Im Thurn that the men follow the water-courses, and thus explore further and further inland while he tried to glean additional information from the natives about this fabulous city that he had heard so much about.

This idea of further exploration was fired by "The Legend of El Dorado", (of which he had recently learnt). Though nothing substantial, he thought that he was in the general area. He therefore sent out sorties of men both to gather information and to learn as much as possible about this fabulous city. The men were instructed that they must enquire as unobtrusively as possible so as not to reveal their true intentions.

In every village the men visited, the inhabitants seemed to have a legend concerning such a fabulous city but never a definitive knowledge of its location. However, whenever they were pressed, they generally indicated that the city is somewhere in a westerly direction and, although they have heard of it, no one has ever seen it or have ever been there, since they cannot eat it if they have it nor wear it, so they never expressed any interest in gold.

This enigma of refusal to lead a party, or having no interest in the yellow metal puzzled Im Thurn. He tried to induce them with trade goods but seemed also to be unsuccessful, which caused some tension between some Chiefs and himself. Another contributory factor that puzzled the Chiefs was that, although the whites hunted the forests and fished the streams, they hardly if ever shared the spoils with the locals. They also refused to work in the fields and wanted to give less and less trade goods for more and more commodities of the Indians.

Im Thurn, as chief of the whites, always imposed himself on the Tribal Meetings sitting next to the Chief. This he did in the guise of learning the language. This however fooled no one especially when the Chief learned of the real motive, the White Men's penchant for the yellow metal. This deceit tickled the awkward bone of the native Chief since openness and honesty are hallmarks of all Indian dealings.

The Chief therefore decided to devise and lay a plan to deliberately mislead Im Thurn when he would next press for information.

Since none of the whites accompanied the natives to their farms, they, the natives, were free to plan and to discuss and tell the whites what they wanted them to hear. They discussed a story they heard and barely remembered from their ancestors hundreds of years ago during their last trek. It was a story partly based on fact, and partly made up. The facts were so old that only snippets could be recalled, of some sort of a reminiscence of a legend.

The Chiefs and Sub-chiefs discussed the *"Tale of the Seven Cities of Cibola"*, which still remained part of their ancestral history. As they refreshed themselves in the crude huts in the farm, they surmised that this story was the most plausible since everyone had heard of it and would be less likely to make slip-ups if inadvertently questioned. This tale fitted their purpose well since the white men were to believe it in its entirety. The Chiefs hoped that the visitors would soon leave them in peace when they heard such a plausibly rehearsed tale of this place more fabulous than the famed city of El Dorado for which they were searching.

One night, when Im Thurn pressed for information (an opening the wise Chief had been waiting for), the Chief gently launched into the prepared tale. The story he related went somewhat like this:

So, one evening when the moon was an opalescent orb in the eastern sky, when the planting of the fields was done, and some of the White men were away on some mysterious adventure, a meeting of the entire tribe was called. Every male was summoned to be present to hear a fantastic story. It was secretly agreed that this story be told for the benefit of the remaining Whites.

As usual Im Thurn was invited and encouraged to bring his diminished entourage since, after the meeting, there will be the usual "manore". When all was settled in, with Im Thurn settled at the right hand of the Chief, the 'kari' bowl was passed around.

Afterward some frivolous matters were discussed and settled as the men somberly passed the bowl along. Then a state of lull seemed to settle on the meeting which Im Thurn took advantage of to broach his favorite topic, not knowing that this situation had been specially orchestrated especially for him and just such a moment. Something important seemed to hang in the air when Im Thurn had spoken. The expectancy now seemed all encompassing. It only needed the slightest prod for the Chief to launch into his tale.

As the Chief, without the slightest twinge of an eyelash or any expression on his chiseled face deliberately and slowly related his tale, the silence became so thick it could have been sliced with a knife. Im Thurn was so engrossed that he seemed to have fallen into a trance and did not 'bat an eye-lid' throughout the rehearsal of the entire tale. Meanwhile, while the other elders of the tribe nodded their silent approval, Im Thurn seemed so enthralled that he could never have even suspected in the slightest that this was a performance for his and his men's ears only. There was an audible sigh as the Chief concluded, *".... and when ours left and entered the Maranon, the people they met did not even want the gold they brought with them in exchange for the simplest of tools, or even in the exchange of food. They (our ancestors), even disposed of their heavy golden ornaments since it chafed their necks and arms in the intense tropical heat among the humid forests and rivers."*

All seemed mesmerized as the Chief concluded narrating his fantastic tale. The bowl of kari was passed around now, as all the men took copious quaffs. When the Chief handed Im Thurn the bowl, Im Thurn asked the Chief, "Can you visit me in my benab tonight?"

"Certainly", replied the Chief after a long moment of hesitation.
When the Chief and Im Thurn left, they slowly wended their way through the bright moonlight to Im Thurn's spacious benab at the edge of the village. This was not the first time the Chief had visited, but he was taken aback when the kerosene lantern was lit to

reveal, beside the usual camp paraphernalia in the middle of the dwelling, a table spread with a white cloth upon which stood two expensive looking bottles and two cups. There were four chairs arranged around the table, but no one else was in the benab.

Im Thurn motioned the Chief to one of the chairs as he took the one opposite and said, "Make yourself at home Touchau".

Silently and effortlessly Im Thurn poured two drinks into two cups from one of the bottles and pushed one towards the Chief. He lifted one cup towards his lips and invited the Chief to do the same.

As the scalding whiskey coursed down the throat of the Chief, his eye started to water. Im Thurn had emptied his cup and put it down, so at the expense of not offending, the Chief did the same, all the time swearing not to undergo such torture again.

After a suitable pause during which time Im Thurn surmised that the liquor must have reached the Chief's brain, he refilled the cups and motioned a second swig. Despite the Chief's promise to himself, he did as he was bid. The first shot had already induced a degree of euphoria in the great brain of the Chief.

Bit by bit Im Thurn picked the brain of the Chief as to the whereabouts of this fabulous place. Im Thurn could elicit nothing new from what has already been said, so he changed his tactic, and asked the Chief if some of the Chief's men could lead him and some of his men to the location. The White man was so intent on getting as much information as possible that he encouraged the Chief to over-imbibe, and before he could encourage the Chief to commit his men, the Great Chief lapsed into incoherence.

After two days had passed and Im Thurn's men had returned with the same negative results; the White Chief summoned the leaders of his expeditions to a council. He related the tale and the council decided that, regardless of how long it takes, they would mount an expedition of all the White men with tribal guides. However, such an expedition required a lot of trade goods and fresh supplies to ensure a successful foray into the interior - for how long no one knew.

Half of the men were sent to the Coast for supplies, while the remainder hunted the surrounding hills and fished the rivers laying up enormous stores of preserved fish and game. Meanwhile, Im Thurn who had failed with the wary Chief, switched to inviting other influential men to imbibe of his limited stock of whiskey. Some of these men later joined by others continued to hang around Im Thurn's benab in the afternoons in the hopes of being offered a drink. After a time, this became a habit amid some of the weaker ones, so they started to neglect to cultivate their fields.

This went on for about a month. After this time the women found it more difficult to cultivate the fields alone, so, securing food for the family became more difficult since even the idle men began demanding more of the household larder than was their adequate share.

The Chief now realized the woeful blight that had now been visited on his village, Arewa, the Big-Fish "The Pride of the Savannahs". He wished that the White men go with their lust for gold. If they leave their debilitating fire-water will leave with them. Think as he might the Chief could not come up alone with a solution, and he dared not call a full Tribal-Council since two of his elders were also hooked on this 'Devil's-brew'. The Chief could not even ask the White men to leave since hospitality demanded otherwise. He then did not want dissention in his camp nor violate tradition. So, he thought that, as soon as the trade goods with the Whites arrived from the Coast, his problem will be solved. He also thought that with the lure of liquor, some of his best men might be persuaded to join the Whites as 'guides' and so leave the village without the best workmen.

Despite his subtle suggestions and harangues at Tribal-meetings, (which not surprisingly were not now attended by Im Thurn, having the information he wanted), the men promised but some still continued to neglect their and filial duties, much to the chagrin of the Chief.

Im Thurn's men returned from the Coast, laden with trade goods and ample supplies of whiskey. This saddened the Chief a great deal, for he knew what this may mean to his tribe. But help came from an unexpected quarter, as Manitou is wont to hear the inner pleadings of His children.

Immediately on their return with the supplies, two of the men came down with a hot fever and with red spots erupting all over their bodies. Im Thurn, aware of the implications, kept his men quarantined in a hut, admonishing them under severe pain of punishment if they even show themselves outside the tent.

However, despite the massive doses of laudanum administered to the two invalids, one of them died. The secret could no longer lay hidden, since, although the Whites tried to bury the corpse during the night, such an affair could not be hidden from the Chief.

Shortly, as word spread about the strange condition of the corpse, four men who frequented Im Thurn's hut fell ill with the same illness. After a week, all four died and a few children of the affected households came down with the identical illness.

At a hastily called Council Meeting, now diminished, secret plans were made, and so, when the whites woke up one morning, there was no smoke issuing from the various benabs of the village. A sortie was sent out after a few days to ascertain the whereabouts of the tribe. They were traced to the foothills of the Kanukus, but as soon as the trackers entered the wooded area, two fell victims to poisoned arrows. This dissuaded any further pursuit, and so the pursuers were obliged to return empty-handed.

Left alone the White-men became a victim of their own sins as they ate into the stocks, both solid and liquid, against the assumed return of the natives. They left after a month, emaciated and greatly reduced in numbers and health. They gathered what they could, moved southward and journeyed over the Acarai into the Amazon region and were lost to all purposes to civilization for many years, until we last heard again from Im Thurn in England.

****

Our Native Peoples

Since the onset of human history when the earth was young, beautiful and unspoiled, when the term "Man" meant Adam, or the Sanskrit meaning of "Adami" or Mankind, when one and all spoke in the plural, meaning all, not merely "me" and "I" as singular the psyche of man was more liberated. His sense of what was good and fair was informed by societal norms rather than self, then love of brother was paramount.

Let me now invite everyone of us to take a minute to introspect, to revert to our inner selves and answer a few questions. I shall now posit. We need not verbalize our answers, but just ponder them in our quiet moments, and then answer them quietly to ourselves. Here are the questions:

"If any of us, cocooned as we are in our cities, engrossed as we are in self, who has lost touch with Nature and the natural world, was to be put in a society that seeks not for itself, will any of us know how to act? If so, how? If not, why not?"

I remember reading a book by Peter Townsend. Peter, some of us may remember, was rejected as being suitable to be married to royalty because he was not of blue blood. In the soliloquy to his

196

book, "Earth My Friend", penned after the rejection, he tried to catharsize because, in order to forget his ladylove, he bought a jeep and travelled around the world, to try to find what he could find. This caused him to visit societies in all stages of development and acculturation. This to my mind, qualified him with timely experience to introspect on the dilemma of, "Who is Civilized"?

"Is it he?" He asked himself, "who was born and bred 'in affluence and culture', or the family in the humid tropical jungles of Central America who, in the middle of the night, who was very gracious to offer him and his entourage accommodation in the middle of the night?' This encounter was unexpected and among total strangers.

"What would he have done if he had discovered that, in the middle of the night, four dirty and half naked savages were walking up his driveway in Brussels?" He answered himself by saying that he would have loosened his killer dogs on them.

I have also read that, along time ago, that, when the then President of the United States of America, asked the Mahatma what was his opinion of Western civilization, He replied that he thought that this was a very good idea.

At this juncture let me categorically state that I am all for civilization, multiculturalism, and acculturation. However the path that the modern practices are embracing to achieve this do not augur well for society as a whole. Just keep the questions and your answers in your mind for silent and sober cogitation.

Let me again ask a few questions. Is giving in to the greatest good for the greatest number, superior to giving in to the greatest good of all? Is this good for the greatest number an evolutionary step laterally, upwards or downwards? It is my thesis, and hence an integral factor of my belief structure that, if a society only caters for only a fraction of itself, then inadequacy is a factor of the system itself, and therefore cannot be superior to a society that caters adequately for all. The simplistic answer that society has grown more complex is inane since, with complexity of problems must evolve complex solutions. If the institutions of development do not develop concomitantly, or evolve concomitant solutions, vis-a-vis, say economic development, then the danger of moving in a negatively skewed direction is ever threatening the system.

With these as my rubric let me attempt a broad perspective of the origin of our Native Peoples.

Some ethnographers subscribe to the theory that the whole of the South American region is populated by people who island-hopped from the Dragon's Mouth from Trinidad into Venezuela or took a western Andean route down to the tip of South America and, therefore, Guyanese Natives are of either Carib or Arawak origin. Others again have traced a more southerly migration route from the Negro and Branco into the savannahs and llanos of Venezuela where sizable chunks of our people have settled. Those who support the migration from Asia during the Bering Strait millennia ago, during the interglacial period, with the eventual spread as far as Tierra del Fuego at the extreme tip of South America, do not account for the migration spread down the Amazon. Whether eons ago a branch left the main body at the headwaters of the Amazon and migrated eventually into the llanos and the Roraima highlands is open to conjecture and future scientific studies.

Whether people crossed from the numerous islands of Micronesia and Polynesia, (where long marine voyages were a way of life), to inhabit the Andean Highlands and spread outwards as theorized by Hyderhal and others, constitutes another school of thought. Whichever is true might be proved in the future, now that the human genome is mapped. But whether such technology will ever be harnessed to trace the genesis and lineage of these most neglected sectors of the human race is a moot question.

I have raised this question of origin, since a people's cultural manifestation does not depend solely of the response to environment, but is founded also on their history and previous response to contradictory and like situations both diachronically and synchronically.

If one were to take note of the difference of the food culture of the South American/West Indians (potato/cassava), and the Meso and North American (maize), fundamental ethnographic and anthropological questions are raised which in themselves need in-depth investigations.

Now, although living among a people gives some insights into their cultural patterns, a really extended period of time is required to really comprehend the subtle intricacies of behavior. The initiated, by observation, discussion, and indulging with everyday mundane activities, go a long way to help one mesh unobtrusively into the cultural tapestry and, thus acquire a deeper, more profound and subtle understanding of the psychology and mores of the people. Anyone who makes it obvious that he is different, he is superior, or even quasi-superior, will readily, upon questioning, given the answers he wants, and not necessarily the truth or the fact of the phenomenon under scrutiny.

If even trained anthropologists and ethnologists can easily miss, how much more will the miss-informed and non-expert - to spread rumors and outright lies of the behavioral idiosyncrasies of people with whom they have barely come into contact with, or people with whom contact was merely peripheral.

An outsider may be told or feel that parents are not very demonstrative to their children. This is very far from the truth since the people are some of most loving, patient and caring parents, especially when teaching some skill or nicety of behavior.

In Guyana, a much-misrepresented behavioral pattern concerns the sexual behavior of these people. They are often portrayed as being promiscuous, or at least of having loose morals, to being individuals of easy virtue. The reality is directly the opposite. Unlike other sects and societies, they are predominantly monogamous.

Both promiscuity and loose morals are taboo and rigorously condemned.

These misconceptions might have arisen because of the many young women who have removed themselves from their villages and sought employment outside with a lure of the better life and who have opened themselves to sexual exploitation by unscrupulous employers and others with evil intentions.

On the other hand, in the villages, male strangers are accepted as "yaku," or brother-in-law, and, though he may not be in any consensual or conjugal relationship with any female in the village, he is required to treat all females as sisters, aunts or sisters-in-law, and all males as brothers, uncles or brothers-in laws.

Intellectually they are second to none, and have proven themselves the equal to anyone as can be validated at institutions of higher learning when they are afforded the opportunity by being awarded scholarships.

As artists and artisans it is safe to posit that, as a percentage of the population, there are more superior ones among the natives than among the general population. In Guyana the various crafts and basketry designs have to be seen to be believed. In this country one only has to visit a pow-wow or the Native Museum in Manhattan to see products of exquisite beauty and of aesthetic excellence.

These Native Peoples hold promises and contracts sacred and will go out of their way to repay a kindness, fulfill an obligation or preventing the letting of one another down. What is humbling, when one gets to know them, is the depths of their moral refinement and the way that they deal with the greatest of tragedies. The latter can only be experienced since it defies adequate description.

On a broader spectrum, these people know little of a holocaust as that suffered. Records were not kept so there is no accurate tally. Little of their sufferings was ever documented, not merely by default but mostly by design. From the very onset of European civilization that was introduced into the Americas, imported diseases played havoc among the Native Peoples. They had no immunity to common diseases, which wreaked havoc among them not only one or two people but, sometimes, entire villages.

Starting in Meso America with Cortez in Mexico, the decimation of whole tribes of men, women and children by soldiers and pioneers continued into North America and persisted until not very long ago by the bounty on Indian ears by the sheep farmers in southern Argentina. These all perpetuated the blatant extermination of entire villages in Amazonia. All these bear brutal testimony to the brutality meted out to these people, and are still being meted out by the hand of foreigners because of greed. Remember the cliche, "Any good Indian is a dead Indian?" Remember most of the American Westerns where the rouges were the natives and the "good guys" the Pioneers?" This is still alive today in parts of South America where Drug Lords and Timber Barons rule. If even some of the atrocities meted out to these people had been documented, it could have been seen to exceed the Jewish holocaust in numbers.

These people have given the Eastern world the staple potato (Batata batata), tobacco, tomato and maize. Their ancestors, the Inca, pioneered brain surgery, predating contemporary scientists. These people pioneered astronomy and, if they had crossed the Pacific, they were the greatest mariners, predating the Vikings and Columbus by eons. The bolas is a very effective weapon used to bring down prey and enemies harmlessly and is still being used by the gauchos of today. Curare or wourali is one of the most studied poisons in medicine. Native South Americans gave this to the Western world. Rotenone and quinine and their derivatives are today universal drugs, while sarsaparilla is a renowned flavoring.

There are many other plants waiting to be discovered in the Natives' pharmacopeia that they have used for years. There are also lore and sagas, tales to be told and endless knowledge to be gained when we get into the psyche of these people. Imagine, the Americans only granted them citizenship to their own country in 1924! These people in their hey-day lived in harmonious symbiosis with their environment and nature. They never polluted nor wasted or ever overexploited.

While I do not advocate returning to a time, which we regard today as primitive, much can still be learned from them, especially the protection and sustenance of the Space Ship Earth. Their unique way of co-operation when work is to be done, is a methodology, (once marginally employed by the Pioneers), can be adopted by developing countries in societies where funds and other resources are scarce and labor and the means thereof are abundant.

Communal work and communal play, breed not only unity but mitigate against selfishness and fosters a lasting love of people, and not a love of things.

(Above: Amerindian Chief – in Guyana – Source: www.en.wikipedia.org)

****

Glossary

Acouri: (*Dasyprocta aguti*) A small brown rodent much prized for its tender flesh. It inhabits the forested and secondary growth areas and also frequent abandoned farms. It is mostly nucivorous.

Adouri: (*Dasyprocta aguchy*) A smaller rodent like the acouri, which it resembles. Edible.

Arewa: The original name of the village Lethem at the confluence of the Takutu and Moco-moco rivers. Now the largest town in Region 10.

Awara: *(Astrocaryum tucumoides)* A tall palm with very spiny trunk. The leaves also have spines. The tree bears golden yellow walnut-sized fruits, in bunches, which are sweet and succulent when ripe. The trees grow well on the numerous sandy reefs in Guyana. The fruit is a delicacy to all animals. It is sought after by humans also.

Arakapusa: From Spanish Arquebus - a gun, especially the flint and pan type.

Anaconda: *(Eunectes muriana)* The largest living snake; an aquatic constrictor.

Benab: Generally, the various Amerindian houses; the temporary ones go by different names.

Bush-cow: One of the names of *(Terrestris americana)*.

Bimiti: Local name for a type of humming bird that builds its nest of soft downy materials over creeks and other bodies of running water. There is lore to say that when the rains are heavy the water will rise but never to touch the nest; literally a flood-barometer.

Cakeralli: Aka Kakeralli (*lecythis ollaria*) A tree in the second storey tropical forest where sunlight is scarce. It grows tall, but where sunlight is abundant like the exposed banks of a river," small gnarled and knotted tree. It has green small leaves with some of various shades of bronze bright red. Its flowers are like beautiful pink orchids. Wild animals find both flowers and fruits edible.

Cassava: Genus *(Manihot)* A tropical American plant with starchy enlarged root; a staple of both The Arawak and Carib cultures.

Cayambay: *(Curatella americana)* A shrub or small tree normally with gnarled branches, with rough sandy leaves and very siliaceous wood. A fire-climax plant found on certain parts of the llanos.

Cokerite: *(Maximiliana regia)* A palm. The trees grow to about sixty feet or more. The leaves are like huge fans and are used extensively as thatch in th savannahs. The fruits are borne in huge bunches of sometimes over 100 pounds. The fruits are purple balls with a thin layer of milky flesh, which is very nutritious and makes a delicious and healthy drink. Both in the savannahs and the forested regions, a part of the young leaves is extracted as (tibisiri), and plaited into a number of utilitarian articles and woven into hammocks.

Congo-pump: *(Cecropia peltata)* Also called the trumpeter-tree; A semi-hollow-trunked tree that grows up to forty feet tall. There are two types, distinguished by their two types of palmate leaves. The dried leaves are brewed into a herbal tea for the treatment of bladder disorders.

Coastlands: The Arabian Coast, which extends from Punta Playa in the North West to the Courentyne River, approximately 270 miles. However only the Essequibo Coast from Charity to Supenaam is known as The Arabian Coast. (Found on old Maps).

Casreep: The boiled down poisonous juice of the cassava after the poison has been extracted by boiling. It evaporates into a thick dark brown 'sauce, ' which both preserves and flavors. Used by all Guyanese.

Chuno: An Andean Staple

Cayman: *(Eunectes muriana)* Also called caiman. The largest Guyanese reptile resembling crocodiles. All four are called alligators by the locals.

Capybara: *(Capybara hydrocaris)* The largest rodent in the world. The flesh is tender and edible and much sought after by lovers of "bush-meat". Live in small flocks and are vegetarians.

Darwan: A temporary fish-basket made on the spot with young ite leaves, either one or two as is required. This is used for temporary transportation in place of the warishi.

Duraquarra: Aka called duraquarro *(Odontophorus guianensis)*; the smallest of the game birds. The early morning call of this bird gives it its name. Onomatopaeic.

Fling-far: The anaconda or camoodi. *(Enectes muriana)*

Farine: Also called farina, literally (flour). Coarse cassava meal made by grating the cassava, expressing the juice, sifting and baking over a slow fire, constantly turning it; a staple among the Natives. Called 'savannah rice' by the Coastlanders.

Gooby: Hollowed out calabashes or gourds used for storage and other utensils.

Gourd: *(cucurbitacea)* A vine; it is related to the squash, pumpkin etc. but has hard outer shell that dries into a durable tough container. The fruits are inedible but the hard outer shells, when ripe, are made into (goobies) and used for storage. The fruits range in size from the peach-size to volumes ten times the volume of a football.

Hiawa: Aka Hyawa. *(Icia hypaphylla)* A large shrub that has a crystalline resin with a very sweet scent; the local incense tree.

Haimara: *(Erithrinus macradon)* A large game fish noted for its fine flesh; sometimes grows to 50 pounds.

Hatie: Aka Hattie *(Hevea sprucena)* A tree that gives off a yellow resin. The roasted seeds serve as bait for certain kinds of fish.

Hurwe: A species of endangered monkeys. (Protected by CITES?)

Ite: Pronounced Aetay *(Mauritita flexulosa)* A palm of fan shaped leaves It is the most useful palm of the savannah. Every part has its specific use.

Iguana: *(Iguanidae sp)* An arboreal reptile. It is prized for its delicate flesh by many. The Carib name is 'waimuka'.

Itabu: A sort of miniature bay in the bend of a river frequented by fish.

Inca: The original people of the Andes. Some anthropologists subscribe to the idea that they migrated in a series of migrations over the Bering land Bridge, while some are of the opinion that they sailed across the pacific from the Indonesian Islands.

Kayap: Another name for Mashramani; a well-known word in the Pomeroon and the North-West Region of Guyana (Arawakan).

Kulasali: (Tardidae sp.) The savannah thrush. A song-bird with spotted breast and brown upper plumage.

Kamma: Another name for the tapir *(Tapirus americana)*.

Kanaima: See Chapter on Kanaima.

Laudanum: Tincture of opium; a cure all among the inhabitants of the interior in the olden days.

Lukanani: A medium sized game fish found in fresh-water creeks. Resembles the rainbow trout.

Manicole: *(Euterpe exharriza)* a medium sized palm that usually grows in clumps up to 50 feet high. The fruits are a favorite food for the toucan and piscine birds; harvested as "The Heart of Palm" and sold commercially in stores.

Manore: Another name for Mashramani; used among the savannah tribes.

Mashramani: Co-operative work after which there is much feasting and drinking.

Matapi: A cylindrical basket made from a reed (mucru), used to express the toxic juice from the grated cassava.

Maipuri: *(Terrestris americana)* another name for the tapir.

Maranon: Another name for some of the upper parts of the Amazon River. Originally the entire river was called Maranon.

Moco-moco: 1. *(Caladium arborescens)* A herbaceous thick stemmed plant that grows mostly in swampy places mostly along river banks. The young leaves and fruit are the favorite food of the Canje Phesant. However this herb is better known for the healing antiseptic qualities of a juice from its bark that speeds the healing of cuts and bruises.

2. The small river, which joins the Takutu River at Lethem.

Monkey-pot: A tall forest tree that bears a foot-ball sized woody fruit. The fruit, when ripe, contains a saccharinous edible content. This is a favorite of all denizens of the forest.

Night-jar: *(Craprimulgus)* the Local 'who-you?' bird; A night bird.

Pipiyo: *(Lapingus cineraecus)* Green-heart bird.

Pura: Incan name for Peru

Powis: *(Crax alector)* A large game bird of the forested region. Resembles a turkey tom with a recurved ruff on its head.

Piaab: Any of a number of small fish used for bait.

Quake: A more or less permanent small covered basket used for the transportation of fish.

Souari: *(Pekea tuberculosa)* Timber tree used for lumber and making boats

Souari-nut: The nut of the souari tree; this nut is considered as the best and most tasty nut rivaling the Brazil nut.

Seven Cities: The famed seven cities of El Dorado of myth of Cibola

Shack-shack: Maracas. Made from small calabashes and shaken rhythmically at music meets.

Tacooba: Aka tacuba (Arawak) The heart-wood of trees after the sap has disintegrated.

Tacooma: Aka tacuma (Arawak) The grub of the beetle *calandra palmarum*. It is considered a delicacy among some natives. The (surum) of the Machusis and Wapishana; "ewoi" of the Carib.

Tapioca: Farinaceous meal made to resemble coarse sago. Made from cassava. It is very nutritious. Used mostly for feeding infants and convalescents.

Taurenero: *(Humirium floribundum)* A large, normally straight, timber tree with red-brow wood and rough bark. Game birds feed on the fruits.

Troolie: *(Manicaria saccifera)* The most popular thatch palm.

Tuma-pot: This term is used interchangeably with pepper-pot.

Touchau: Leader of the tribe

Too: *(Ramphastus toco)* The largest toucan; usually found in pairs or threesomes.

Supplementary Reading

1. *"The Discoverie of Guiana"* Sir Walter Raleigh; Sir Walter Raliegh

2. *"Green Mansions,"* WH Hudson

3. *"The Kon Tiki Expedition,"* Thor Hyderdahl

4. *"The Rivers Ran East,"* Leonard Clarke

5. *"Wai-wai,"* Nicholas Guppy

(Amerindian children: Source: www.inewsguyana.com)

9 781717 584199